D1060577

JOAN COLLINS
Superstar

JOAN COLLINS
Superstar

A Biography

Robert Levine

Weidenfeld and Nicolson · London

Published by arrangement with Dell Publishing Co. Inc.
Published in Great Britain by
George Weidenfeld & Nicolson Limited
91 Clapham High Street
London SW4 7TA

ISBN 0 297 78657 1

Printed and bound in Great Britain by
Butler & Tanner Ltd, Frome and London

For Mom and Dad, who are really wonderful.

Contents

Foreword

When one decides to write a biography of Joan Collins, one is faced with an interesting life; a not (until recently) particularly interesting career; and a fascinating, complicated woman. Earlier in her career Joan always seemed to be working at cross purposes with herself; in the past two years, however, she has become a spokeswoman of sorts for women over forty-five years of age, and that is but one of the niches she has found that suit her perfectly. Her starring role in ABC's *Dynasty* has totally rejuvenated a career that even at its best was never thrilling, and she recently posed, with great success, for *Playboy*. She has helped prove to the world that women over 'a certain age' can be immensely attractive.

Hollywood glamor photographer George Hurrell was chosen to take the black-and-white series of photographs that appeared in *Playboy*. Hurrell, a veteran of over fifty years with Hollywood studios, has photographed Garbo, Dietrich, Harlow, and hundreds of other stars. Mario Casilli, one of the most sought-after celebrity photographers in the world, was responsible for the color photos. He recalls the impression Joan originally made on him when they met years earlier. 'It was 1956 or 1957. ... She was much more quiet at the time and was nowhere near the lady she is now. I was impressed with her then, but I would never have guessed that she'd become such a star.'

Joan Collins became a star despite, rather than because of, her career. Overcoming the frequent comparisons that have been made over the years – first to Jean Simmons, Ava Gardner, and Jane Russell, and later to Elizabeth Taylor – Joan has remained entirely memorable for who she is. The impression she managed to make on people from the first time they saw her was indelible. Initially these comparisons severely impeded her movie career, but they never diminished others' awareness of her as a person, as an individual. It is not surprising that Joan's appearance in *Dynasty* pushed the show from the thirty-eighth position in the Nielsen ratings into the top ten, and occasionally into the number-one spot. She had been an active part of moviegoers' unconscious for over two decades.

In the 1955 crime melodrama *Tight Spot*, Ginger Rogers has a line that goes: 'Television should be so good that when you close your eyes it sounds like a radio.' With Joan's clipped speech, perfect diction, dramatic timing, and almost audible sneer, one hardly has to watch her to know what it is any scene she's playing is meant to convey. The fact that when one does get to see her one's breath is taken away is almost, in theatrical terms, a bonus. Joan's attention to detail would seem to be better suited to the small screen. In this respect she is very much like her good friend Robert Wagner, since he, too, managed to get lost on the big screen. Joan Collins in the comfort of one's living room somehow seems larger than she ever did in the movies, and her dynamics can be seen in a finer perspective.

In 1958, in an interview with Louella Parsons, Joan discussed the lack of glamor in contemporary movie stars in contrast with Gloria Swanson, Marlene Dietrich, and others. She asserted that these legendary ladies had something different from what was currently seen on the silver screen. One suspects she was referring to 'presence' or 'image', both of which are components of glamor. '[Joan] follows in the tradition of the stars of yesteryear,' Mario Casilli said at the end of 1983. 'She has an image and she knows how to exploit it. It's almost as if she's a product.' What Casilli is talking about is what Joan was talking about – that almost intangible thing known as 'star quality'.

I have attempted herein to present Joan Collins as accurately as she has always presented herself. Movie stars have the added burden of having to grow up under public scrutiny, and Joan has, finally, risen to the occasion. She was always better and more dramatic off-screen than on. Great actresses make even the small roles seem great. Stars, on the other hand, make, almost accidentally, their smallest movement off-screen seem like the apocalypse. When Joan broke up with a boyfriend in the fifties, it was in public. He called her a 'fucking bore' and she called him, immediately, a 'boring fuck'. Recently Joan sat feverishly at the bedside of her comatose daughter for weeks, working against what the doctors told her were the girl's slim chances for survival. She worked for her daughter's life and won. If the two events seem to be contradictory, that is because they are. Large personalities don't fit into neat packages unless they're manufactured, and Joan was unlike the other starlets of the fifties, many of whom were manufactured. Hollywood never quite knew what to do with Joan. The people in charge of the studios tried to fit her into one of the many slots they had for actresses – sexpot, lady, weak-willed woman, unhappy wife. Joan simply wouldn't fit. She was, as it turns out, too multifaceted. That may well be why she has survived.

We are all subject to the genealogical throw of the dice, and Joan is no exception. She seems to take after two female members of her family – her mother, who was a doormat, albeit a loving doormat, of sorts; and her paternal grandmother, an emancipated woman who had no fears about speaking her mind and living life to its limits. The combination leads to frequent self-contradictions, and Joan Collins has lived almost fifty-two years trying to prove that, in fact, there's nothing wrong with the occasional self-contradiction. She has tried valiantly to solve many of her personal problems, in particular her self-denigrating relationships with men, which she sees, I think accurately, as being rooted in her relationship with her father.

When the time came, Joan exploited her image as a sex symbol rather than have it exploit her. Now, it seems, the world has caught up with Joan Collins. She always liked sleeping with men she found attractive, she always had a nasty mouth, she never saw herself as a complacent housewife, and she was always into 'image'. Even her type of vulnerability has become fashionable. She has lost at love all of her life, but has lost none of her love for the concept of love. She is still a hopeless romantic, waiting for the right man to come along and make things right for her.

At this point in her almost thirty-five-year career, Joan Collins is a greater star than she ever dreamed she would be. She is comfortable in her dual role of mother and actress, and is successful at both. She has grown up – 'Britain's Bad Girl' of the fifties has proved that she is a real survivor. The contradictions remain and make her the fascinating woman she is.

I

First Breaks, First Mistakes

As an infant Joan Collins was so beautiful that perfect strangers were always trying to kiss, hold, steal, or adopt her. With the exception of the last two on the list, little has changed in almost fifty-two years.

Joan's whole family was good-looking. Her mother, Elsa Bessant Collins, was part French, a blond, blue-eyed beauty, with strong Anglo-Saxon features. Joseph William Collins, her father, was Romanian-Jewish, with a strong profile and handsome features. He had curly black hair that he always wore slicked back and parted in the middle. Although he was only five feet ten, he seemed in many ways to be a giant to Joan. He frightened her and was prone to wild fits of temper. He was the object of all of Joan's affections. Of the relationship between her parents, Joan recalls, '[Mother] was such a slave. She thought of herself as secondary to Daddy. She didn't stand up for herself.'

Joe Collins (known professionally as 'Will' Collins), was a theatrical booking agent, in business with Lew (later Lord Lew) Grade, the British film producer. Grade is Joan's unofficial godfather. The Collins home was always full of theatrical types – ventriloquists, comedians, singers – who told Joan often that she should be in show business. And why not? She was adorable, sang all the time, and had come from a family of performers. Her paternal grandmother, Henrietta – Hettie for short – was a dancer who performed professionaly up until a month before the birth of Joan's father. She was an uninhibited vaudevillian known for her high kicks and splits, which both shocked and delighted the staid Victorian audiences of her time. From all reports she was sassy and rebellious – another pair of traits that found their way into Joan's personality. Grandma Hettie encouraged and paid for Joan's dancing lessons from the time her granddaughter was three years old.

It was apparent from the beginning that Joan loved to perform. She excelled at dancing school, appearing as a fairy in the school's show shortly after she began her lessons, and later, at the age of six, performing splits taught her by her grandmother. Also, at the age of three or four, Joan went with her mother to a London department store. Elsa Collins remembers hearing laughter, and when she turned around, there was baby Joan entertaining the shoppers by trying on hats and imitating the postures of grown-up models.

Joan's father had two sisters. One, Pauline, was also a theatrical agent; the other, named Lalla, became a dancer. All the women in the family agreed on two things – that Joe was irresistible and that Joan should keep out of show business. No one in the family – with the possible exception of Grandma Hettie – wanted Joan to become a performer; they knew the business from the inside and thought it was far too rugged and with too little chance for success.

Born on May 23, 1933, Joan Henrietta Collins was the Collinses' first child, and Joan had Joe to herself for almost the first five years of her life, until sister Jackie was born. When Joan was seven, the Second World War began to take its toll on London, and the family was evacuated. The Blitz disrupted their lives as it did the lives of millions, and the frequent relocations, with the accompanying change in schools (thirteen in all!), neighborhoods, and faces, turned the outgoing, gregarious Joan into a shy, if still beautiful, young thing.

'I scarcely ever slept a whole night in one bed,' Joan later recounted. 'I was [always] being awakened and carried to an air-raid shelter.' Once, after a bomb hit their building, Joan recalls going back to her nursery. It looked like 'a giant matchbox – nothing but splinters'. At the seashore she and Jackie were forbidden to go into the water for fear of detonating a mine. The family had to sleep in the London subways occasionally while the Germans were bombing. It was a hideous time for Joan, who slept for years with her bedroom door open and the living room light on to ward off the old fears.

During the war years Joan was often asked to help her mother in the kitchen, but she took badly to housekeeping. 'Joan did *not* inherit my love for housework and cooking,' Elsa Collins wrote years later. 'You know, Mummy,' Joan would say to her, 'you chose to be a housewife. I didn't. You chose your career. I have chosen mine.' That career was to be an actress; earlier interests, such as illustrating stories written by sister Jackie, were gone by the time the war was over.

Joe was away during most of the war. He had a business to run, and the demand for variety shows during the war was earning him a respectable living. To Joan, however, his absence implied abandonment. Possessed with the insecurities of childhood, she couldn't imagine why he would be away from her if he really loved her, she had been his darling, his angel. First Jackie had come along, then the war and his frequent long-term absences. What could have gone wrong? What had *she* done wrong? Many first children feel displaced by the birth of the second, and Joan seems to have had trouble adjusting to the change.

By 1945, when Joan was attending the Francis Holland

School, she was, by her own admission, pimply, gawky, and withdrawn. She was pale and thin, sported a dutchboy haircut, and was made to wear a drab grey school uniform that didn't help matters. 'I wished I was a boy during puberty. I hated the whole idea of becoming a woman. I was quite keen to become masculine,' Joan now says. She dreamed alternately of being in ballet or of being an artist, romantically living in a garret. She had no interest in school subjects and wanted to be through with Latin and mathematics as soon as possible. Good marks, she felt, would 'only get you squinty eyes'. The drama course at the Cone-Ripman School offered some respite from the doldrums of schoolwork, however, despite the fact that the drama teacher told all the girls that none of them had what it took to become an actress. It was through the school that she got her first acting job, in the London Arts Theatre production of Ibsen's *A Doll's House*. Joan played Nora's son, Ivan. Her part was tiny – only one line – but she managed to screw it up anyway. She was reading a magazine backstage and missed her cue twice, throwing the rest of the cast off their cues and driving the director to swear that he'd never use children in his productions again.

'At least when I was acting I could play a part,' she explains. More to the point was the fact that as if Jackie and the war hadn't been enough, Joan was now faced with another, more formidable, rival for her father's affections. The Collinses had a third child when Joan was twelve, this time a boy, Bill. Suddenly he was getting all the attention, and Joan therefore decided that she, too, would become a boy. She went with her father to football matches and pretended to have a great time despite the fact that she hated watching sports almost as much as she hated playing them. It did, however, give her a chance to be near Daddy, and that was the object of the charade. It didn't work, of course; Bill still got the attention, and Joan concentrated on becoming an actress.

At the end of her final school year Joan made a fortuitous decision when she applied, against her father's wishes, to the Royal Academy of Dramatic Arts. She read scenes from *Our Town* and Shaw's *Cleopatra* for her audition and waited weeks for the Academy's decision. Fifteen hundred children auditioned and only two hundred would be accepted. 'Let her take the exam; she'll never pass it. It will be the end of it . . .' Joe told Elsa Collins. But Joan did pass, and was accepted. Father and daughter made a deal: He'd pay the tuition for two years, but if by then she showed no progress, she would look for another career, probably in secretarial work.

That summer, when Joan was sixteen, the whole family went on holiday to France. Joan fell in love with a French boy named Bernard whose father owned a few ice cream shops. This was Joan's first real opportunity to spend time with a boy, since none of her schools had been coeducational. Bernard couldn't speak English and Joan spoke no French, but somehow they communicated, eating ice cream and strolling on the beach.

At the Academy that fall Joan continued with her discovery of boys, developing – according to her own accounts – an enormous need and desire to lose her virginity. She later referred to herself during this period as a 'P.T.,' or Prick Teaser, but in retrospect it appears that the boys presumed she was teasing when, in fact, she was deadly serious. A twenty-two-year-old fellow student, who was probably homosexual, became Joan's steady. 'Nice girls' at the time didn't go 'all the way', but Joan apparently wanted to nevertheless. The two of them carried on as much as they could, given his inability to actually do what had to be done.

He, it seems, was not acknowledging his homosexuality, and his anger over his own confusion and with Joan's needs, which he couldn't fulfil, turned him sadistic. He bit and grabbed, he punched and kicked. All his frustrations were taken out on her, and – true to form – she felt it was her fault. He was to remain unattainable, like her father, and seeming like all the other boys she developed crushes on. One day he reportedly suggested that Joan go to bed with his roommate. She unexpectedly agreed, throwing them both into a panic. 'Nice girls' were supposed to protest, but Joan called their bluff. Her suitor became furious, called her a slut and a bitch, and dragged her into the bedroom himself. At last, Joan thought, 'it' was going to happen! But as usual, he couldn't do what he wanted to do, and Joan wound up being bitten and hurt.

He apparently did love her, though, and that counted for a great deal with Joan. Her mother had been telling her for years that sex was no good and that the word *fuck* was so bad that if Joe were ever to use it, she would divorce him. It appeared to Joan as though she would never find out about sex for herself. But while her sex life was getting nowhere, there were career developments that would eventually lead somewhere.

2

Britain's Bad Girl

Joan began to model. An agency had come to the Academy looking for girls to do some magazine work. Joan was one of the two chosen. She liked and needed the money and used it to attend the theatre, her real love. She had spent the previous summer with the Maidstone Repertory Theatre as third assistant stage manager and had acted as promoter for six plays. She understudied parts in four. The theatre had become her passion and her ambition. Slightly annoyed at the way she was being treated by the Royal Academy, whose instructors seemed to feel that she had little talent or potential, she was grateful for the chance to be photographed. Many of the photographs for sensational crime magazines found Joan as the girl about to be raped by a lunatic in a haunted house. Away from the camera she began wearing lots of makeup and affecting tight black turtlenecks handed down from her theatrical Aunt Lalla. Those efforts got her noticed and photographed in trendy jazz clubs, which had become another of Joan's passions.

An agent named Bill Watts spotted her and suggested that he try to get her some work in films. Joan was going through what she refers to as her 'repulsive period' at the time. The crowd she ran with was called 'the slobs'; they were artsy and bohemian and cared little about their appearance, as long as it spelled rebellion. They all frowned on filmwork – it was too commercial; the proper goal for an aspiring actor or actress was the stage. Joan, however, was bored with her classes at the Academy and it showed – she had been cited as a bad example to others because of her lack of interest in her schoolwork. With nothing to lose, she decided to give filmwork a try. At that point she was eighteen, normally a time of blossoming beauty for young women. Joan, however, had been staying out drinking and smoking in jazz clubs until far too late, and she was overweight. Watts reprimanded her: 'Your hair's too long and needs a shampoo; your dress could stand a pressing; and you're much too dirty.' In addition, she was pimply, a condition Joan speculated would disappear as soon as she lost her virginity.

Joan had to cut classes in order to take her screen tests, which got her into more trouble at the Academy. She tested for the lead in *Lady Godiva Rides Again* and won a tiny supporting part. (She's not even listed in the credits.) The whole experience bored her, but she went out again for a film called *The Woman's Angle*, this time getting the part of a Greek maid, for which she was paid fifty pounds – enough at least to keep her in costume jewelry and turtlenecks. She posed for more pictures. The British press took to her at once, comparing her favorably with Jean Simmons, Jane Russell, Lauren Bacall, and Ava Gardner.

The director of the Royal Academy let her know how he felt about filmwork – it was nonsense to him – but by this time Joan was beginning to feel the same way about the Academy and its attitude toward her. Defiantly she threw herself into her new role of movie starlet; at least she was appreciated, and occasionally adored. Everyone needs his ego stroked, and Joan was no exception, no matter how sophisticated she was made out to appear. She decided to forget about her abusive boyfriend and concentrate on herself. Ten years later Joan heard that he had become an actor and had had a breakdown on stage, after which he had never been the same again. At least she hadn't married him.

An undistinguished film called *Judgment Deferred* came next, but it was important to Joan's career. Ealing Studios noticed her in it and called her in for a test. After three tests she landed the part of Norma, a reformed prostitute, in Basil Dearden's *I Believe in You*. Her co-star was Laurence Harvey, who was to become a good friend. Dearden was a successful and well-respected director who had previously scored big successes with *The Blue Lamp* and *Kind Hearts and Coronets*, and according to Bill Watts, whoever was cast in his new film was bound for stardom. It was her first big break, and Joan was thrilled.

All this time Joan continued to live at home with her parents, dating a lot and spending hours on the phone. Sister Jackie used to listen in on Joan's conversations and report her every move to their parents. Eventually Elsa Collins had to remove the extension phone to give Joan some privacy and curb the heavy sibling rivalry that was brewing.

During this period Joan attended lavish parties frequently escorted by Laurence Harvey. Although he and Joan were only friends, Hermione Baddeley – the woman with whom Harvey was living at the time – believed the relationship to be otherwise. She was suspicious and jealous. According to Joan, at one party which she and Harvey attended together, Baddeley attacked Joan verbally, telling her that she had neither talent nor guts. Joan left the party in tears, demonstrating, at least for the time being, that the second accusation was close to the truth.

It had now been a year since Joan's picture had first appeared on the cover of a magazine. During that time her career had started to take off; people had begun to notice her. One of them was the Irish actor Maxwell Reed. He had long been one of Joan's idols, and when they met through Laurence Harvey he thrilled her by asking her out. He was thirty-one (she was eighteen) and very handsome. She was living with her parents and didn't dare tell them she had a date with a man almost fourteen years her senior, so she lied and told them she was going to a party with Laurence Harvey.

She met Reed at the appointed place and went for a drive through London. By her own account, Joan was all nerves – would she bore this older, more worldly man? Was she dressed properly? Would she say the right things? As it turns out, these were the least of her worries.

Joan had thought that they were going to one of the private clubs London was so filled with in the early fifties. Instead they wound up at his flat. Reed announced that he was going to take a bath and made her a drink to 'relax her'. He gave her something to read while he was getting ready, and sipping her drink, Joan gazed in absolute horror at what he had given her. It was illustrated pornography – drawings of men and women having sex in positions Joan had never imagined.

Joan's next recorded memory was of waking up with her clothes ripped off, her body racked with pain, and the sheets stained with blood. She had been throwing up. She had been unconscious for three hours. And she was no longer a virgin. She passed out again and when she came to, Max was trying to put a 'strange soft object' in her mouth. She staggered to the bathroom and was sick again. She passed out again and woke up periodically until 3 A.M., having been repeatedly raped. Her mother had often warned her that 'men only want one thing', and now Joan realized that she had been drugged in order for Maxwell Reed to get that 'one thing'.

Finally he took her home, carefully leaving her at the door. There she confronted her parents, who were by now close to hysteria. They had checked with Laurence Harvey when she wasn't home by a reasonable hour and he had told them that he hadn't seen her. Her father was in a rage, while her mother attempted to comfort her. Joan lied again – she said she had been with a friend. Once more she was believed, but she wished she could tell her mother the terrible truth. Sadly, Elsa Collins was so weak and frightened of her husband that she repeated whatever confidences she was told, so there was nothing for Joan to do but to lie and keep her humiliation inside. Joan's feelings of love for her mother were tinged with a real lack of respect for her in those days. Three hours later she was on her way to the studio for that day's filming of *I Believe in You*, no doubt a little tired, more than a little confused, and most significantly, no longer a virgin.

Oddly, inexplicably, self-deprecatingly, Joan continued to see Max Reed. Her father had treated her mother badly, so wasn't that the way of the world? The man called and the woman jumped. Joan was still a long way from being her own person, particularly with men. She blamed herself partly for what had happened – after all, a nice girl wouldn't have wound up in a stranger's flat at night. Neither of them discussed that eventful evening, and Reed treated her politely and with respect. When they had sex, Joan found that she was bored or annoyed, but she went along with it. She was remarkably naive for a girl who pretended to be a real hot number and who was being touted in the press as a British version of Jane Russell or Ava Gardner. Deep thought and introspection apparently were not part of Joan's daily routine, and the public image of her and her own private self-image had nothing to do with each other. She threw herself into pretending to love Max, pretending to enjoy sex, but the only things she apparently genuinely enjoyed were making *I Believe in You* and posing for publicity shots.

The J. Arthur Rank organization, one of England's hottest movie companies, was interested in Joan and soon signed her to a seven-year contract. The press followed her everywhere.

When *I Believe in You* opened, the notices were good; *Variety* said that Joan turned in a 'strong, dramatic' performance. In contrast to *Lady Godiva Rides Again*, which Joan herself calls 'wretched', this was quite a step up. Her career was taking off. The British magazine *Film Review* wrote of Joan's early performances, 'If she is as good as she is believed to be, then almost inevitably we shall lose her to America.' The press was ahead of Joan on this point – in 1952 Hollywood was the farthest thing from her eighteen-year-old mind.

Joan continued to shield her parents from the truth about her relationship with Max. They were convinced by him and by Joan that the two were just professional friends. All the while their romance continued, albeit with some kinks and problems. Max was often in pain as the result of a slipped disc and this severely impeded their love-making. Joan relates that he began to beat her in order to become sexually aroused, and Joan, once again presuming that it was her fault – as were all griefs suffered by men, weren't they? – agreed to his perversions. She posed for some nude photographs for him, which he kept. He told her it was her job to understand the pain he was in, and indeed she tried. It was true that he hadn't made a film in months, and he made Joan feel guilty for his problems, especially in light of her success. He and his friends even suggested that Joan became a high-priced call girl – *courtesan* was the word they used. The not very emancipated Joan found the whole thing amusing. At that point in her life, however, Joan and her feelings were such strangers to each other that they might just as well not have inhabited the same body.

When Joan first told her parents of her plan to marry Reed, her father stalked out of the house, leaving his daughter in tears. He returned hours later and comforted the still-weeping Joan. He eventually gave in, but with the warning that if the marriage didn't work out, he'd never want to see or speak to

Joan again. Disregarding her father's warning, she and Max got married the day after her nineteenth birthday. Inwardly she must have known that the marriage was a big mistake, a catastrophe, but if she couldn't make Daddy adore her, at least he would have to take notice of her. Attention is, after all, attention, whether it's negative or positive. She remained afraid throughout the marriage – afraid of failure, afraid of upsetting her father, and, most of all, afraid of Max. Max belittled her in public and told her that she, like all women, would be washed up by the time she was twenty-three. Viewed today, in light of the way Joan's career has worked out, the remark is both ironic and amusing. It wasn't at the time.

Joan was interviewed by the London *Daily Mirror* and declared that she had no intention of cooking and cleaning, and that her career was of the utmost importance to her. For the 1950s, this attitude was practically blasphemous, but it helped Joan's image as 'Britain's Bad Girl', 'The Coffee House Jeze-bel', and 'The Pouty Panther'. And it got her plenty of publicity.

The honeymoon was awful. Max dyed his hair and wore makeup to look younger and flew into rages every time he suspected that Joan was looking at another man on the beach at Cannes. They fought constantly. Luckily Joan was signed to start work on *Decameron Nights* – another, as it turns out, totally forgettable film – to be filmed in Spain. The high point of her trip to Spain came when she was almost arrested for wearing extremely tight jeans on the street. She returned to Max and their fighting began anew.

Another movie came up for Joan, *Cosh Boy* (released in the United States as *The Slasher*). In it she played (again) a wayward teenager, this time getting pregnant and attempting suicide. The film proved to be popular in a sleazy sort of way, although it was not exactly a milestone in her career. At least it got her away from Max for a time. It was filmed on location, in Italy, and at one point a still-naive Joan found herself surrounded on the beach by a huge crowd which had massed to stare at her in 'the first bikini seen locally. For all my bluster, I turned around and fled,' Joan said later. Joan seems to have been very adept at getting herself into situations she couldn't handle.

Together the Reeds appeared in *The Square Ring*, which, in addition to practically chaining Joan to Max, also did nothing for her reputation as an actress. The newlyweds also appeared together in several stage plays. In *The Seventh Veil* Max had to slap Joan's face. He did so once with such ferocity that he knocked her halfway across the stage, leaving her black-and-blue for a week. A while later, appearing in another play, *Jassy*, Joan got to return the favor, slapping Max. Little did the audience realize how close to real life their performances actually were.

Max finally got a role in a production without Joan and she appeared in some plays without him for which she got relatively good reviews. Next there came a film called *Turn the Key Softly* in which Joan payed a young prostitute. By then, however, Max was back on the scene and their tortured life together continued. Their dinners reportedly consisted of Joan cooking badly (which she admittedly still does to this day) and Max throwing the food across the room, leaving Joan to pick it up. Apparently she was finally sick of being married to Max but was too weak and insecure to do anything about it. Plus there was her father's threat hanging over her. What would it take to make her leave Max?

Meanwhile, her less-than-spectacular career continued. Next came a film called *Our Gal Friday* (released in the United States as *The Adventures of Sadie*) in which Joan played the part of the only female survivor of a shipwreck, washed up with three men. Once again it got Joan out of London and away from Max for a while, so it wasn't a total loss. *The New York*

Times succinctly – and somewhat unkindly – summed up Joan's performance in this film:

> Joan Collins is perfect for the bikini suit in which she swims and in which she undulates across a beach. And she doesn't make a bad impression in a tattered dress either. She makes no impression as an actress.

'I rebelled at being cast externally in "bad-girl-goes-downhill" roles because even a moron could see it was killing me as an actress,' Joan told an interviewer two years later. She hated the roles she was getting, but had been typecast by the studio and the industry. The studio suspended her once, angered by her refusal to continue to do stereotypically tawdry parts. But she was still only a young starlet and had little autonomy or authority to command meatier parts.

Joan went back to theatre work after *Sadie* and played a Byzantine empress who makes love to young men and then sends them away to be executed. The play was called *The Praying Mantis*. It was Joan's first 'killer woman' role – laying the foundation for a characterization that was to culminate some twenty-five years later in *Dynasty*'s Alexis Carrington Colby.

In the 1954 Lewis Gilbert film *The Good Die Young*, Joan was wildly miscast as the middle-class, long-suffering pregnant wife of criminal Richard Basehart. She was dreadful in the part – perhaps the character's suffering reminded her too much of her own life with Max for her to work up the necessary steam for it.

The irreversible event that made Joan realize that she had to get out of her marriage came one evening at a posh London club. She and Max were sitting at their table, enjoying their drinks and the music, when Max became involved in an animated discussion with a man at the next table – an Arab sheikh. Max asked Joan to dance. Once they were alone on the dance floor, Max communicated a deal the sheikh had suggested. It went this way: The sheikh would go to bed with Joan – for one night only – Max could watch, and Joan and Max would get paid £10,000! Joan was disgusted, furious, and horrified. She screamed 'Never' at Max and stomped out of the club. It was the first time in her life that she had been so assertive with a man, but finally she had meant it. She had walked out and this time it was for good. She feared what Max would do – he had threatened to have her face cut up if she ever left him – but no matter. She just wanted out, and she got out. She went home to live with her family and closed an early, ugly chapter in her personal life.

Out of the ten pictures Joan made for the Rank organization, nine were loan-outs. The last one was to Warner's, and it proved to be a turning point in her career. They needed someone to play the sultry, sexy, evil Princess Nellifer, who 'claws her way to the throne' in *Land of the Pharaohs*. Six months earlier Joan had been testing for a picture in Paris when director Howard Hawks met her and spoke to her for five minutes. When he called six months later, Joan was appearing in a play; he gave her three days to make up her mind whether or not she wanted the part of Nellifer. She grabbed it and flew off to Rome, where much of the film was to be shot. Darryl F. Zanuck, then head of Twentieth Century-Fox, was in Rome at the time and spotted Joan. He was looking for someone to replace or at least challenge the rebellious Marilyn Monroe, who had recently walked out of Fox – again. He was knocked out by Joan. 'That girl acts with the authority of a bullwhip. And besides, what a face and chassis!' was his recorded reaction. He at once began negotiations with the Rank organization to buy her contract.

Land of the Pharaohs was undoubtedly the movie that first introduced Joan Collins to American audiences. The press releases were wonderfully lurid: 'Her Treachery Stained Every Stone of the Pyramids,' the ads read. It seemed as if it would be a great role; director Howard Hawks had been a Hollywood figure since 1918 and had made such films as *Sergeant York*, *The Big Sleep*, and *Gentlemen Prefer Blondes*. The scriptwriters were William Faulkner and Harry Kurnitz, so there were great expectations. The dialogue, however, turned out to be ridiculous (and it wasn't enhanced by Joan's too-British accent). The resulting film was a critical shambles. Joan, however, was 'discovered' and immediately compared to Elizabeth Taylor. All the comparisons Joan was getting turned out to be a mixed blessing – throughout her movie career, she kept reminding people of other stars, and it is only recently that she has found her own niche.

While Joan was filming *Land of the Pharaohs*, she fell in love. Her co-star was Sydney Chaplin, second son of the great comedian Charlie Chaplin. Joan had had very few laughs – or even light moments – in the past year, and Syd had a great sense of humor and told endless, screamingly funny stories that kept the cast and crew in constant laughter. He kept Joan amused and happy while they were in Rome. They even laughed for hours in bed. Syd referred to himself as a 'funny fuck', and while Joan says that this isn't altogether true, she does admit that their lovemaking often ended in hysterical laughter, with one or the other breaking into a full-fledged comedy routine. They raced all over the Italian countryside in his sports cars, and it was precisely the type of fun and excitement that Joan needed. One has the feeling that Joan had decided what it was she definitely did *not* want – that being Max Reed – but that she hadn't figured out what it is she *did* want. She was twenty-one years old, in the process of extricating herself from a nightmarelike marriage, and not making any long-term plans for the moment. She and Syd ate and drank to such excess that they could hardly fit into their costumes; at times they laughed so hard on the set that filming had to be stopped dead in its tracks. None of this made Hawks particularly happy.

Max was also filming in Italy at the time and the estranged couple met on the beach one day. He told Joan that he wanted money and jewelry in exchange for the nude photographs of her he had taken. She was terrified; not only were the photos embarrassing, but the fifties' attitude was very moralistic and this sort of exposure could ruin a budding career. Fox was still in negotiations with Rank to buy Joan's contract and it was just the break she needed. She gave in, agreeing to Max's terms. He did not live up to his side of the bargain, however – he kept the pictures. Joan's mother was with her in Rome at the time, and accustomed as she was to one type of abuse or another she managed to be a great comfort to Joan.

Joan was offered an exclusive seven-year contract with Fox at $350 a week. She turned it down. Not only did the money seem like far too little (she wanted $1,250 a week), she felt bad over the prospect of leaving Syd. She and Syd went off to visit his family in Switzerland and she met his famous father. Syd refused, for some reason, to sleep with her in his father's house, however, and this totally threw her off. Typically, of course, she put up with it.

They drove back to Paris and discovered that her demands had been met by Fox. There had been a nine-month hiatus between *The Good Die Young* and *Land of the Pharaohs*, and Joan realized that the British film industry had no idea what to do with her. With few regrets, therefore, Joan left her family, lover, friends, and familiar haunts and memories and flew almost immediately to Hollywood. The British press gave her an enormous send-off. Internally, however, Joan was faced with a real dilemma: She was being given exactly what she had been asking for, and now she had no idea whether she really wanted it.

3
A Babe in the Woods

Joan landed in New York on her way to Hollywood in November of 1954. She discovered 'slot machines' that dispensed candy and cigarettes at the drop of a coin, and also discovered that at the drop of a few coins in the Automat one could purchase an entire meal. She was so much like Alice in Wonderland that she wound up spending all of her money and got to Los Angeles without a cent in her pocket. 'A nice studio chap' who met her at the plane had to lend her fifty dollars just so she could take care of some basic necessities. She was very impressed with the informality she found in the United States. 'America is wonderful. The people are so friendly. Why, they call you honey or sweetie five minutes after you've met them,' she commented to an interviewer at the time.

Her reputation as something of a vamp had preceded her. While filming *Land of the Pharaohs*, she had mentioned to a publicity man the fact that her mother had had to put a sign on her pram reading 'Please don't kiss me' when she was an infant. For some reason this piece of news became twisted, and she had become known as the 'kiss girl'. As a result strange men in Rome began grabbing and kissing her and news of this arrived in the States just as she did. The fact that she admitted to wearing 'bikini bathing suits just to shock people' only added to her image as a sexy rebel.

She moved into the Beverly-Carleton, an apartment house with no dining room, and spent far too much time alone. She was lonely and knew no one. One night she walked for miles looking for a restaurant and was accosted by a man who grabbed her arms and wanted to talk to her. She was scared but spoke to him. He eventually tipped his hat and left, and Joan ran back to her apartment.

She tested for weeks for a part in a film called *Lord Vanity* opposite Robert Wagner, who was then one of Hollywood's leading young heartthrobs, but she was eventually told that she was too young for the part. Feeling miserable and lonely, she hopped a plane for Paris to be with Syd Chaplin to 'forget all about Hollywood and [her] disappointing career'. She returned with 'five bags of trash', having shopped Paris clean.

By June 1955, Joan was famous enough, without ever having appeared in an American movie, to be lengthily interviewed by both *Photoplay* and *Motion Picture Magazine* in articles set to appear in their September issues. In September she appeared on the cover of *Life* magazine and had a three-page spread in *Look*. The Fox publicity department was doing a spectacular job of marketing her, but they couldn't get her to fit into a mold. *The New York Times* movie critic had hardly greeted *Land of the Pharaohs* with great enthusiasm. 'Joan Collins,' he wrote, 'is a torrid baggage in filmy costumes who obviously is equipped to turn a potentate's head. Her acting never does.' Joan, herself, told *Look* that she was 'perfectly awful' in the film. In fact, she spoke a bit too much of her mind to keep the publicity people happy. Her favorite recipe, she told *Look*, was 'a can of beans and instant coffee'. She desperately wanted to be taken seriously as an actress but had no idea how to go about it. Her great desire was to get some good acting roles in a hurry. All the reviews from her British juvenile delinquent films had played on how sexy she was and the press coverage she was getting in Hollywood did the same thing. Her appearance, her style, and the interviews she was giving didn't help. She was specifically told by the Fox publicity people not to speak to the press about anything of any substance, i.e., religion, politics, etc., and so she found herself left with the most remarkably banal things to say.

Sidney Skolsky, in the *New York Post*, asked her what the greatest struggle in her career was. 'Getting into a tight evening dress,' she responded. 'She sits with match sticks on her eyes to make them more luxurious – "another trick Grandma taught me," ' the interviewer continued. She has the 'face of a pouty panther, wears gold nail polish with gold sandals'. Rumor has it, Skolsky went on, that 'ex-King Farouk used to send her a dozen roses every day'. Joan did not quash the rumor. She added that she 'once wore a dress so tight-fitting'. she 'had to be carried upstairs'. *Motion Picture Magazine* reported that 'Joan also loves snug matador pants in orange or shocking pink that look as if they've been put on with a spray gun. She stuffs her cigarettes and matches into her bra, and her open shirt makes it easy for her to reach for a smoke.' These were not the sort of interviews that would get the studio to consider Joan for the title role in *Medea*.

The whole country knew her measurements (38″–23″–37″, just for the record). But Fox didn't know what to do with her and neither did she. 'She may be the heat wave that will shake Marilyn Monroe to the very tips of her pink toes,' *Photoplay* announced. She 'could fill in for any of Mickey Spillane's sultrier heroines'. Her beauty was touted all over, and that easily could have been enough for her. A few months before, Joan had ben voted the girl with the most beautiful face in England. Her father was asked to comment: 'I can't see that,' he said. 'She's got a nice face and a nice personality, but I wouldn't say that she was particularly beautiful.' Years later Joan said she wished her father could have conceded and told the press that she was 'wonderful and beautiful and gorgeous'. Even her beauty wasn't being acknowledged by her father; what more could she do? She couldn't please herself and she couldn't please him.

But the press genuinely liked her. Her warmth and innocence came through despite the inanities of her remarks and manner of dress. 'She has a candor that is completely disarming,' one reporter stated. 'This girl has no postures. She is incapable of pretense.' When Joan spotted a story about herself in a press release from Fox, 'she yelped like a kid'. Directors found her easy to work with, but the reporter aded that 'if she ever becomes aware that she's a living bonfire, only the Good Lord knows what will happen'. She was an anomaly, *Films and Filming* pointed out in December of 1955. She was the first of the British actresses *not* to be one of the 'ladies', like Greer Garson, Merle Oberon, Vivien Leigh, Audrey Hepburn, and Deborah Kerr. The United States, it was clear, would simply have to look upon her in a whole new way.

Syd came to Hollywood to live with her and brought with him a ring, earrings, and bracelet of topaz and diamonds for Joan. Meanwhile, working at last, she busied herself making *The Virgin Queen* with the awesome Bette Davis. Most of the attention was naturally focussed on Davis, who was recreating the role of Elizabeth I, one that she had first assayed in the 1939 film *The Private Lives of Elizabeth and Essex*. Joan played the lady-in-waiting whom Sir Walter Raleigh loves and marries. She was, according to the *Times* film critic, 'pretty and mildly vivacious, adequate to the plot'. It was a case of damning with faint praise, but things were happening so quickly that it hardly made a difference to either Joan or her career.

The next role for which she tested was the title part in *The Girl in the Red Velvet Swing*. Joan wrote home to her sister Jackie, almost daily, asking her to 'keep praying for me' to get the part. She was thrilled to announce this to an interviewer and asked if the interview would really be printed. 'Just wait till Jackie reads it!' she said with glee. Jackie, seventeen at the time, wrote constantly, asking for all the Hollywood gossip, and Joan supplied it happily.

The role of Evelyn Nesbit Thaw, the glamorous turn-of-the-century chorus girl whose husband murdered her lover in a fit of jealous rage, was supposed to go to Marilyn Monroe, but she wasn't interested in it. Many young starlets tested for the part and Joan worked dedicatedly on her American accent. She landed the part, and with it came a spate of publicity the likes of which she had never imagined. She posed constantly, 'dressed as an Easter bunny or a Thanksgiving turkey or a big valentine'. The fan magazines were so full of her that she could barely get away from herself. She was seen spending lots of money, with fives and tens always falling out of her purse. She bought herself a mink coat and a Ford convertible, the former dark brown, the latter bright pink. She moved into an 'elegant apartment' for £250 a month(!) in Westwood. Her 'innocent voluptuousness' was turning her into a wealthy woman.

Syd wasn't working, and his enforced idleness put an enormous strain on their relationship. He stayed home and watched television or went out drinking with friends. One evening he was supposed to pick her up, in her car, at the Palm Springs airport. She arrived and he was nowhere to be found. She finally found him, drunk, in a bar. She yelled at him, he ignored her. 'Fuck you, Sydney! Fuck you! Fuck you! Fuck you! Fuck you!' she yelled. 'And fuck you too, honey,' he replied. 'That,' Joan answered calmly, 'is the last time you will ever fuck me.' And that, as they say, was that. The chapter of her life having to do with Sydney Chaplin came to an abrupt close.

One of the men Joan had met through Syd was Arthur

Loew, Jr., whose father headed MGM. He and Joan began to date. Joan had been out with very few men other than Syd (and occasionally his brother, Charles Chaplin, Jr.) and it was time for a change. She and Arthur became an 'item', and he squired her all over. He accompanied her to New York for a publicity trip for *The Girl in the Red Velvet Swing*. The movie was a minor success, and Evelyn Nesbit herself commented to Joan and the press about how lovely she found Joan. The reviewers didn't agree. They praised her beauty, but found her performance wanting. 'She manages to make the soapy clichés sound even more sudsy than they are,' one reviewer noted. Once again, it barely mattered. Joan was looking forward to her next film, which was to be either a remake of *Jane Eyre* with James Mason (it never got made) or *Boy on a Dolphin* (the part went to Sophia Loren). *The Girl in the Red Velvet Swing* opened in October of 1955, and Joan was on her way to London for the first time in eleven months for the opening of *The Virgin Queen* and her sister, Jackie's, birthday. She carried with her lots of presents: 'plastic shoes with glass heels, a gold purse, lipsticks, nail polish, and lots of records – Jackie is jazz-happy.' She said it was easy to buy gifts for Jackie, her mother, and her young brother (Davy Crockett paraphernalia), 'but I never know what to get for my father'.

While in New York she talked to reporters, did a TV show, and pressed a button that turned on a new lighting system in the Bronx. She 'looked like a siren but conducted herself like a lady', *Photoplay* said. She has 'stood the test' of a star, they reported. Her outfit was designed for her femme fatale image, like Mata Hari. Her makeup was like Theda Bara's. 'Joan Collins had taken the trouble to look like the kind of star she is supposed to be.' Comments like these lead one to the realization that Joan knew that she, personally, was going to have to make up for what the studio and her pictures weren't doing for her.

Part of this self-knowledge was probably due to the fact that Arthur had convinced Joan to go into analysis. He had been in analysis for years himself and was sure it would do her some good. She began to discover that 'stardom' was empty, and that becoming a whole person was far more important. She learned, or started to learn, to live each day as it comes, and to enjoy what happens. Early in 1956 columnist Hedda Hopper wrote about Joan that 'she [looks like] she combs her hair with an egg beater'. This was because when Joan wasn't being a star – on or off the screen – she dressed down, and went out, simply, as Joan Collins. The hustle and bustle was confusing to her and she was trying to sort it out. In the early part of 1956 Joan was voted 'most promising actress' three times. Joe Hyams, interviewing her in the New York *Herald Tribune*, quoted her as saying: 'I'm afraid I'll be a has-been before I'm finished being promising.' Joan was aware of what the game was, but was having trouble playing it by the rules. With regard to her acceptance speech for the award, she told Hyams: 'When I was making that phony speech thanking my fans I was worried that perhaps I didn't have enough sincerity in my voice. However I really am gratified that the fans liked me enough to choose me for an award, but everything about the giving and getting of it seems so fake.' Her statement is nothing if not confused and self-contradictory, but it's clear that Joan was beginning to sort out the real from the fraudulent, the genuine feelings from the painted-on smile.

In the months since she had left England Joan had given little thought to Max Reed. While still in London, she had tried to file for divorce but had discovered that British law prohibited divorce until the marriage had been in effect for at least three years. And so the man who had drugged, raped, attempted to sell, and had blackmailed her was still her husband. On March 21, 1956, the New York *Daily News* ran the following story, accompanied by a photograph of Joan as the sultry, sexy Princess Nellifer:

> JOAN'S MATE ASKS ALIMONY
>
> Los Angeles, March 1 – Joan Collins's estranged husband today asked that the pert British actress pay him $1,250 a month separate maintenance. English actor Maxwell Reed, 31, who charged cruelty and desertion in his Superior Court suit, said that he earned less than $1,000 in the past year and was now unemployed.

The British press quoted Reed as saying, 'I made her a success. I loved her. She left me to go to Hollywood. Now I can't get a job.' There was apparently no end to Max Reed's sleaziness.

In May, a week before Joan's twenty-third birthday, Earl Wilson reported in the *New York Post:*

> Miss Collins is off to Hollywood to take up the matter in a divorce action, and we anticipate more durned fun. Funny thing is, he's a prominent British actor, and when she was a schoolgirl, he was her pinup boy.

Funny thing indeed.

A week later, in the same column, Wilson quoted Joan's reply to a question about her marriage to Reed: 'I used to do everything anybody told me was wrong,' Joan said, 'and *everybody* told me this was wrong.' Especially her father, one might add.

Joan was in genuine emotional pain from the entire experience and it was being perceived as 'fun'. To make matters worse, she herself was being flippant about it. She was still afraid of being 'too serious' with the press. But such was the role of the starlet. Arthur Loew gave her a white mink stole for her birthday. It did little to alleviate the pain, however, despite the delight the press seemed to take in the events.

Joan secured the aid of Fred Leopold, a well-known divorce lawyer. He advised her to pay Reed and get the marriage and accompanying torment over with, once and for all. Terrified at what Reed might do – he had, after all often threatened to have her face slashed – she moved in with Arthur. Eventually Max settled for a lump sum of $4,250, in addition to the $1,400 in their joint bank account in London. Joan was stuck with the four-thousand-dollar legal fees as well. Luckily Fox gave her an advance on her salary so she could handle it. Finally she was completely free of Max Reed.

4

The Romantic Life of a Starlet

Joan's father came to California to visit her late in 1956. She wasn't able to meet him at the airport when he arrived, but she sent a note and a friend to pick him up. She and he and Arthur had quiet dinners together, and little of Hollywood's glitz and glamor got through to Joe Collins. When he returned to England, Elsa Collins asked him about Joan's housekeeping. 'The maid's doing a beautiful job,' he responded.

Prior to her father's visit Joan had been busy appearing in *The Opposite Sex*, a remake of the controversial Clare Boothe story *The Women*, originally filmed in 1939. She wrote home often, and Elsa Collins remembers receiving this letter:

> Dear Mummy and Daddy,
> Sorry for not writing sooner and this is just to say that all's well. Will get off a long letter within a couple of days, but right now I'm exhausted. Spent the dreariest day in the bathtub, wearing long underwear.
>
> Love
> Joan

In *The Opposite Sex* Joan played Crystal, a two-timing chorus girl (a part played by Joan Crawford in the earlier version), and in one of the movie's more notorious scenes she was required to take a bubble bath. Shooting went on for so long that Joan developed a rash and had to complete the scene in a pair of men's long underwear. The studio added musical numbers and men to the original script, but the movie wasn't the success they had hoped. 'Eye filling but hardly inspired,' was the way *The New York Times* felt about Joan, but their memories were still with the originator of the part, Joan Crawford, and the much less experienced Joan was bound to pale by comparison. It marked something of a breakthrough for Joan, however, insofar as it was the first 'woman', in contrast to 'girl', she had played in a Hollywood film.

In September of 1956 Joan told Earl Wilson that she wanted to wait a year before she married Arthur Loew so that they could have 'time to curb their impulsiveness'. She added, 'I'd hate to be one of those girls with four or five husbands.'

Joan was smarting from her recent grotesque divorce and was feeling even less secure with men than usual. The relationships she had been involved in had all been bad—her father had been tyrannical; her boyfriend had been incapable of loving her and had treated her sadistically; Max had been, well, Max; Sydney had been fun, but he hadn't really cared about her. And now her relationship with Arthur was turning sour as well.

Joan's next acting assignment was to be *Sea Wife*, co-starring Richard Burton, and filming was to take place on location in Jamaica. Joan loved Arthur enough to want to marry him. He owed her nothing and she owed him nothing; she had remained totally independent financially and they were having fun together. Joan was, and is, a rather well brought up, conventional girl; and felt that marriage should be the end result of any good relationship. She explained to Arthur that while they were separated from each other during shooting of *Sea Wife* they might want to see other people, since there were no ties. She was being indirect and he didn't pick up the hint; he merely suggested that she *not* see other men while she was away. What Joan wanted was to get engaged, but Arthur couldn't believe that a woman who had been divorced for only 'five minutes' would want to marry again so quickly.

'You mean you want to fuck around?' she asked.

'Let's play it by ear,' he responded after a while. She agreed to 'try' to be faithful to him but she went off to Jamaica intending to hurt him. She was angry and disappointed – as she had been with all the men in her life – but now she was a big girl and could do something about it.

Sea Wife was one of the truly unrequited-love stories of all time. Joan played a young nun marooned on an island with three men after their ship is torpedoed by the Japanese in 1942. She doesn't let on that she's a nun because one of the men is a rabid atheist. The Burton character falls in love with her and she claims that she's promised to someone else. When they are rescued and return to London, he sees her but doesn't recognize her in her sisterly regalia. It was an incredibly bad piece of casting on Fox's part and the British press had a field day. The *Daily Mirror* referred to Joan as 'Sister Sizzle'.

During the filming Arthur wrote often, professing his love, and Joan fended off the off-screen advances of Richard Burton. Burton had rather remarkably explained to her that eventually, no matter how hard they protested, he always went to bed with his leading ladies! Joan found Burton arrogant and couldn't believe that he was behaving as he was, especially since his wife was on location with him. Joan turned out to be the exception to Burton's claim. She never, as it has turned out, went to bed with someone in whom she wasn't genuinely interested, and that includes studio heads, influential directors, and egocentric – albeit attractive – leading men.

Arthur showed up in Jamaica and he and Joan spent a

happy if meaningless week together before she had to fly to London for eight weeks of postproduction work. In London she moved in with her parents and received letters from Arthur claiming he would force himself to show her his feelings. As Joan puts it, 'I felt ... sadness ... that I chose to love someone who had to force himself to show his feelings.' It was beginning to sound like an old, old story.

When *Sea Wife* opened, it was seen mostly as a bore, and few of the critics had anything at all to say about Joan. She was being kept exceedingly busy with both her personal and professional lives, but neither seemed to be going in the direction she had hoped.

After a few weeks with her family, living in her old room (which Jackie had taken over in the interim but which was vacant because Jackie was in Hollywood attempting to follow in her sister's footsteps), Joan returned to Los Angeles. She and Jackie were seen at all the best parties. Joan was a star – at least in Jackie's eyes – and Jackie was known as 'Joan Collins's sister'. Their only real physical resemblance was around their beautiful eyes and the incredible bodies everyone seemed to notice. Jackie had, by then, already had her nose bobbed and had appeared in a few British movies that made Joan's early films look like *Gone With the Wind* and *Citizen Kane:* films such as *Undercover Girl* and *Passport to Shame.* She had gotten the leads in 'B' movies and bit parts in better movies, and was trying her hand at Hollywood. She was offered a contract by Fox, but there was a mix-up over union cards and work permits for foreigners, so Fox put her in a charm school instead. She very much wanted to be a star and posed, as only the Collins girls could, in tight sweaters and skimpy outfits. Stardom eluded her in America, however, and she didn't stay long.

Joan's relationship with Arthur was, by now, more of a sister–brother relationship than anything else and Joan was becoming increasingly aware of how important sex was to her. True to her anger with Arthur, she later confessed to having a brief fling with a young man in Jamaica during the filming of *Sea Wife* and to having loved the sheer sexuality of it. Given her earliest experiences with sex, Joan had come a long way.

Her next film was to be *Island in the Sun* and it was to be shot in the West Indies. Joan starred in this adaptation of Alec Waugh's best-selling novel along with Joan Fontaine, James Mason, and Harry Belafonte. The director was Academy Award-winner Robert Rossen, and the production was overseen by none other than Darryl F. Zanuck himself – the man who had been instrumental in bringing Joan to America in the first place. The film itself was a popular, if not critical, success. 'Not a very good script, was it?' Joan rhetorically asked *The New York Times* on October 27, 1957. The reviews confirmed her suspicions. *Time* magazine said that Belafonte performed like a 'talking totem pole', and Joan was referred to only as 'another temptress'. The *Times* called the movie 'dramatically murky and slow', and said about Joan merely that she and Stephen Boyd 'play wanly with a vapid upper-class love affair'. Clearly there was little real drama going on in front of the cameras. Most of it, we later learned, was going on behind them.

Joan had found herself wildly attracted to Belafonte from the moment she laid eyes on him. She was aware of his reputation as a womanizer and was very wary of men who were 'overly conscious of their sexual power'. She also knew that an affair with a black man could ruin her career if it became public knowledge. As it was, the whole discussion of interracial love affairs, which was at the film's core, was still very much taboo. Many states had already sworn not to show the movie. It was the late fifties and Joan was still conventional enough to know better than to try to buck the system. Her sense of the dramatic, particularly off-screen, didn't lean toward blatant self-destruction. And so she and Belafonte flirted madly. Their flirtation was picked up by Zanuck, who himself had had his eye on Joan for quite a while. One afternoon, in fact, he grabbed her and told her to stop wasting her time with 'boys'. 'I've got the biggest and the best. I can go all night and all day ... You need a real man,' he told her. Joan, sickened by the mere concept of going to bed with Zanuck, got out of his clutches and kept out of his way for the remainder of the filming.

She and Belafonte continued their flirtation, but the time was wrong, the situation was wrong. Perhaps they were both stinging from their last relationships. Nothing came of their flirtation – then.

A few months later, at his invitation, Joan went to Belafonte's opening at the Coconut Grove in Los Angeles. The 'King of Calypso' held court in his most captivating manner. Joan was knocked out by his sexuality, but still frightened. A few days later they wound up at the same party, made the necessary small talk, and ended up together in Joan's apartment – and, more specifically, Joan's bed. She claimed he had the most beautiful body she had ever seen, and was taken with the similarity of their color, rather than the difference. The affair didn't last long – practical matters such as their separate careers, different races, and the fact that he was married, convinced Joan that it should end as quietly as it has begun.

After *Island in the Sun* Joan co-starred with Jayne Mansfield in *The Wayward Bus*, an adaptation of the John Steinbeck novel. In it she played Rick Jason's (the busdriver's) alcoholic wife, and the two had some steamy love scenes together. It seems that the whole idea of casting Joan and Jayne together was a big publicity stunt – put two of America's best-known sexpots in the same movie and you won't be able to keep the crowds away. Whatever the philosophy, it didn't work. The critics called it trite, finding the acting on the level of a touring stock company's. Fans stayed away in droves and it flopped at the box office. Joan told Louella Parsons the following year that it was one of her favorite pictures, probably because the role of an aging drunk was meatier than most of the fluff she was normally offered and it gave her a chance to show off her acting talents. In the same interview Joan said of Jayne Mansfield, 'If [she] would stop trying to be so glamorous all the time, she would probably be a good actress.' The comment sounds like the kind of press Joan would have liked for herself; earlier she had complained of always being typecast. Joan's sympathies with Jayne were far deeper, one feels, than even she was aware of.

If on-screen Joan's performances were consistently mediocre, her off-screen performances were minor masterpieces. On New Year's Eve, 1957, Joan and Arthur attended a party together. They began arguing. The fight escalated and Arthur screamed 'You are a fucking bore!' at Joan. She came back instantly with 'And you are a boring fuck!' It was the sort of good-bye that is usually final, and this one proved to be no exception. If one were to gather together 'Joan Collins's Greatest Scenes', this surely would be among them.

In the early part of 1957 Joan kept herself very busy. The New York *World Telegram* reported that she went out with fourteen different men on fourteen consecutive nights, among them, Michael Rennie, Buddy Bregman, both Chaplins, Bob Wagner, and Nicky Hilton. Hilton was recently divorced from Elizabeth Taylor and was a very eligible bachelor. He was reputed to be a genuine eccentric as well as an athlete in bed. Joan has reported he kept a scoreboard next to his bed that he marked each time he reached orgasm! He was spoiled and temperamental, played with guns, and took far too many pills. Like Belafonte, he was a sexy, entertaining interlude for Joan, but she knew better than to get involved with him. He eventually died of a drug overdose. If one were to chart a course for Joan's love life, one would have to say that while she always looked for rocky seas, she tried her best to avoid icebergs the size that had sunk the *Titanic*.

It had been a while since Joan had been genuinely in love. She had no regrets about the young, attractive men she had been dating and/or sleeping with, but she was looking for something more substantial and involving. In addition, she was pretty sick of being labeled a 'tramp' because she slept with men she liked rather than with studio bigwigs who could help her career. The latter was relatively common practice in the fifties – the casting couch was alive and well – but Joan found it an appalling and demeaning practice and stuck to her guns.

While on location in Japan for the filming of *Stopover Tokyo* (which Joan referred to as *Stop Overacting*), a male friend took Joan to watch a live sex show – an orgy type of event. It revolted her. She was celibate for weeks and decided that she liked her sex straight and that it was never going to become a spectator sport, at least not for her. She had, after all, once been offered £10,000 to make love to a stranger while her husband watched, and she had turned it down. She was a normal, red-blooded young woman, and she too often found herself in the crossfire of the hypocritical fifties.

The interviews she gave in 1958 exemplify the confusion she was going through. In March she told the New York *World Telegram:* 'A man should dominate the woman. Not push her around, but he should wear the pants. American women are too aggressive and that's not feminine.' In the May issue of *Photoplay*, she was quoted as saying, 'I resent the freedom that men have ... They can go anywhere they want and do as they please ... Girls are forced to take subtle measures to get the right man to ask her for a date. I hate playing games and that's what it comes down to!' She defended her defiant attitude toward life, claiming that she was sick of always being criticized.

'While Joan has been establishing herself as a star, there is a question whether or not she has found herself as a person ... She is like a perky poodle, constantly tugging at a leash,' Carl Clement wrote in *Photoplay*, and he seems to have hit the nail on the head. She was torn between the way she was thinking and feeling and the way she suspected she ought to be thinking and feeling. It took twenty years, women's liberation, and the sexual revolution for the rest of the world to find out what Joan instinctively knew in the late fifties. The fact that she was not permitted to act on her instincts was a constant source of torment for her, and it did nothing for her career. 'If you don't mature as a person, how can you mature as an actress?' she asked in the New York *Herald Tribune* in July, announcing that her rebel days were over. Having spent $20,000 on clothes in the last year, she had given up her toreador pants – a sure sign, Joe Hyams, the interviewer, felt, of her maturation. But Joan still had a long way to go before she would really mature, either as an actress or as a person.

Sometimes self-contradictions are the only method by which one can survive, and Joan was proving, less than five years into her career, that she had every intention of surviving.

5

The 'B' Movie as a Way of Life

Joan had made eighteen movies between 1952 and 1957, and despite the fact that she had 'stood the test' of a star, she was still considered a starlet by the studio. In an article titled 'What's Wrong with Me?' in the November 1957 issue of *Photoplay*, writer John Maynard referred to Joan as one of the 'most seen young personalities' on the screen. Joan was railing against never having established a real personality on screen (although, a couple of years before, she was railing against having a juvenile delinquent personality on screen – once again Joan knew what she did *not* want but couldn't get a handle on what she *did* want). 'No one would recognize me in two pictures in a row,' she said, continuing with a complaint about her lack of identity as a star. She had ruled out television in an interview with Earl Wilson, saying, 'I suppose it's great for old people who can't go out, and for kids. But I'd sooner play cards, or *anything*.' Ten years later, and more importantly and significantly, twenty-two years later, Joan would change her tune.

Neither the movies Joan had made nor the performances she had given in them had been particularly distinguished. She was a household name, all right, but no one in America was sitting around waiting for the next 'Joan Collins movie'.

With the exception of her most avid fans, who were more interested in stars than in movies or acting, it was impossible for anyone to get a real fix on who or what she was, and what impact, if any, she was having on the movie world. In the meantime, Joan waited anxiously and impatiently for two things: a career with some importance, with some substantive roles, and an intense love affair.

There seemed to be little she could do about the career. In *Stopover Tokyo* she was called 'pretty and appealing' by *Newsweek*; the other reviews were similarly uninteresting. In rebuttal, she defied Joe Hyams in the New York *Herald Tribune* to 'find another actress who could do better in those parts in those pictures'. She was angry. 'I was as good as I could be in parts that were eminently unsuited for me.' She claimed to be 'very good' as an actress, but as yet the public had no tangible proof of it. She was still under contract to Fox and certainly didn't have the clout – or reputation – to demand better roles. And so she did what she was told.

Doing what she was told was apparently Joan's style, especially if a man was giving the orders. Much of this trait goes back to her trouble with her father. He had, after all, made her promise to give up acting after two years at the Royal Academy if she didn't do well, and to take up secretarial work in its stead. She *was* going to be an actress – to be defiant – if only to prove to him that she could. She was endlessly spunky and outspoken, but like most women with deep-seated desires to please their fathers, she invariably needed a man around on whom to focus her attention. Her pattern was to come on strong, pursue the man, and then become his slave, responding to his every whim. She once said that she liked women with 'balls', but clearly that was true only up to a point, and not necessarily applicable to her.

What Joan needed now was a great love affair, one that would occupy her emotionally, satisfy her sexually, and take her mind off her displeasure with the direction her career was taking. Given her psychological makeup, it is clear that the only other thing that would be a necessity in a new love affair was the certainty that it wouldn't make her entirely happy.

And she found it. There are certain ways in which women can make sure they're going to get into real emotional trouble. Ask any woman and she'll tell you that the best bet is to fall in love with a married man, one who has been married for a while and has at least two children. It can happen, of course, without warning. A woman can meet a man at a party or at a dinner with friends, find herself attracted to him, and fall in love. He can neglect, for whatever reason, to tell her that he's married. She can find herself hooked in no time. This, however, was not the case with Joan's love affair with George Englund.

Joan and Englund had known each other since Joan's arrival in America. He was a friend of both Sydney Chaplin and Arthur Loew. Joan and Sydney used to travel with George and his wife, actress Cloris Leachman, to Tijuana and Palm Springs. The Englunds had three sons; they were two, four, and six years of age. Joan was friendly with Cloris; she was equally friendly with George. Their marriage didn't strike her as perfect, but then again, most marriages aren't. Besides her brief fling with Belafonte, who was married but separated, Joan had made a decision about going out with married men. It simply wasn't for her. Like sleeping with producers, directors, or other studio executives to get a good part, sleeping with other women's husbands was unthinkable and off limits. She was being conventional, but she was also being wise. It was bad news and could only lead to misery. It was obviously the next step.

Joan was on her way to New York to do some publicity for *Stopover Tokyo* and George mentioned casually that he would be in New York at the same time. Why didn't they have dinner together? Perfectly innocently, but probably unconsciously looking for trouble, Joan agreed. They met at the Plaza Hotel and went on to a quiet supper club. By her own account, he was one of the most elegant, charming, well-spoken, and witty men Joan had ever encountered. (Could she have missed this in their two years of friendship?) She fell madly in love and threw caution, conventionality, and common sense to the wind. They spent three glorious days together in New York. He repeatedly told her that his marriage was on its last legs. She wanted to believe him and she did.

They continued their affair back in Hollywood, meeting clandestinely several times a week. Joan confided in a friend who advised Joan to get out of the relationship fast, if for no reason other than that she and George were astrologically incompatible. Joan, who normally accepted the advice of astrologers (and still does), even ignored that warning. She devoted herself to him and became friends with Marlon Brando, one of his close friends. The gossip columnists linked her to Brando romantically and Joan was pleased that it took attention away from the *real* affair she was having. Cloris was suspicious and even showed up at Joan's apartment one night and pounded on the door. The couple cowered under the sheets, not making a sound.

Joan found Englund to be jealous, possessive, and unreliable. He had a wife. In short, he was ideal. They sneaked off to the Caribbean together and he talked about Cloris and the kids. Joan blamed it on herself – the old story again.

Months went by while Joan was between assignments, all the better to obsess on this new relationship. One evening Joan decided to check out the sleeping arrangements at the Englunds'. George had told her that he and Cloris were in the midst of a trial separation and were sleeping in separate bedrooms. Joan sneaked up to the house in the middle of the night (almost getting arrested in the meantime) and discovered that there was no spare bedroom for George to be sleeping in. At her next afternoon tryst with George she confronted him about the sleeping arrangements at his home. He told her that Cloris was pregnant. Joan screamed and threw things at him; never had she felt so abused and betrayed, at least in recent memory. Feeling battered, she was wide open to suggestions that would help her feel better about herself.

Help came from the most unlikely source. Over lunch one day Zsa Zsa Gabor had told Joan that she knew a man who was wildly interested in Joan. He was Rafael Trujillo, Jr, son of the dictator of the Dominican Republic, and he was dying to meet her. The prospect of a blind date 4,000 miles away didn't particularly appeal to Joan, but the idea intrigued her. After her fight with George she called Zsa Zsa. 'I'm leaving for New York tonight,' she said. 'Tell your friend Mr Trujillo to meet me at the Plaza.'

Rafael Trujillo, Jr, twenty-nine at the time, was quite a guy. Handsome, wildly rich, elegant, and accustomed to getting what he wanted, he was recently separated from his wife, Octavia, who had borne him six children. He had given Zsa Zsa a Mercedes and a chinchilla coat, but the press was reporting that the real love in his life was Kim Novak. At the time, this appeared to be true. It also appears not to have troubled Joan, who was in the mood for some revenge, fun, and ego-building.

She soon found herself on board his six-million-dollar yacht, the *Angelica*, moored off the coast of Florida, surrounded by the rich and powerful of Palm Beach, a band, an attentive crew, exquisite food and surroundings, and a man who paid great attention to her and seemed willing to give her anything. Englund seemed, finally, like a bad gamble; Trujillo was no gamble at all. They went to bed together and Joan flew back to New York the next day, not particularly eager to see him again. However, Trujillo's famous generosity did not suffer a lapse with Joan either. The following day in New York, Joan received a necklace sent via Van Cleef and Arpels from Trujillo. It was a diamond choker with several flower-shaped clusters. It weighed twenty-five carats. She kept it.

She stayed in New York for a while and dated the son of a Greek shipping tycoon. She almost convinced herself that partying, diamond necklaces, and an upcoming role in *Rally 'Round the Flag Boys!* would take her mind off George Englund. Joan's mode of operation seems to be to get involved, get hurt, get out, swear never to make the same mistake again, and then start all over. This case proved to be no exception. She left New York with a new diamond bauble from the Greek lad and flew to Los Angeles.

Well on the way to emotional recovery, Joan received, a day after her return to Los Angeles, a single red rose with a note saying simply 'Forgive me. G.' He called often and she gave in. He told her that Cloris had lost the baby and that he had moved out of the house. He told her he wanted to marry her. He had filed for divorce but had been warned by his lawyer not to be seen with anyone, least of all Joan, whom Cloris was hot to name as corespondent. Thinking of her career and her ecstatically happy life ahead with George, she agreed to complete discretion. They went to out-of-the-way places and never got caught together.

Everything was working like a charm. Joan was in love and at last had found a role she wanted to play, a role that made her comfortable. She told Joe Hyams in the New York *Herald Tribune* on August 20, 1958, that the character she plays in *Rally 'Round the Flag Boys!* 'is what I would like to be. [She's] terribly uninhibited . . . completely irresponsible. Nothing, but nothing, fazes her.' Her earlier roles she described as 'dishwasher parts'. 'You wait and see,' she told Hyams. 'I'm ideally cast.'

She turned out to be right. The movie lost money and the

critics thought it was fluff, but they loved Joan's broad sense of humor as the small-town seductress trying to lure Paul Newman away from screen wife Joanne Woodward. In one scene Joan shows up in Paul's hotel suite in a negligee and Joanne walks in on them. (Twenty-four years later *Dynasty* daughter Fallon walks in on a half-dressed Alexis, but the effect was meant to be, and came out, quite different.) Joan was proving that she was good at comedy; maybe the studio would sit up and pay attention.

Fox was a real mess in the late fifties and didn't take the hint. Joan was considered for the title role in *Cleopatra* and was told to slim down for the tests. ('Liz wasn't exactly sylph-like when she played it eventually,' Joan has since said.) Spyros Skouras, a top Fox executive, tried to get Joan into bed in exchange for the part, but Joan refused to break her rule about swapping sex for roles and finally she lost the part. As we know, *Cleopatra* turned out to be one of the most lavish clinkers of all time, and so little by way of career was actually lost.

George became increasingly jealous of all of Joan's involvements, whether real or imaginary. He promised marriage to Joan as soon as his divorce came through. One evening they were together at a party and Joan was wearing the necklace Trujillo had given her. A friend – one of the few who knew where it came from – commented on it. George became livid; he hadn't known about it. He called Joan a slut and ripped the necklace from her throat. Throwing it across the room, he left in a rage, leaving Joan to pick up the dozens of tiny diamonds that had come loose when it broke. Public humiliation was a new wrinkle in Joan's relationships, and she was appalled.

She forgave him, of course. She apologized for sleeping with Trujillo while he, George, was at home with his, at the time, pregnant wife. And he apologized for losing his temper. The whole thing came to light again when news of Trujillo's lavish gift-giving got into the papers, and she and George fought some more.

She was in New York for a few days and happened into Jolie (mother of Zsa Zsa) Gabor's jewelry shop on Madison Avenue. She spotted a piece of costume jewelry that looked exactly like the necklace Trujillo had given her and she bought it, paying $125. She realized she could get some excellent use out of it. One evening, back in California, she and George were walking along the beach and she was wearing the imitation. Of course George thought it was the real thing and she sweetly confessed that she had been very upset over the way he felt about it. With a wave of her hand she tore it from her neck and tossed it into the water. 'I know how much it upset you,' she said, 'and I want you to know that your love means more to me.' He was, understandably, very moved, and the two embraced. It was her greatest performance to date.

George's career was beginning to take off, at last. He was scheduled to produce *The World, the Flesh and the Devil*, and perhaps the newfound success gave him the extra security he needed to treat Joan as indifferently as he treated Cloris. He was cheating on Joan and she caught him. He denied it. She tried to understand; her love for him was that deep. Her sense of self-respect was floating back down the drain; she was the victim again. She was still trying to get her father to love her enough, but he never would. Her life as a doormat for men was continuing on schedule, but unlike her mother, she was finding no happiness in any other area either.

The Bravados, a western (Would Fox never learn? Would Joan?), was to be her next film. She was afraid of horses. 'I think it was a marvelous western, but I genuinely feel that a girl is out of place in a western. She's only put in for the sake of the sexy ads,' Joan told Sheila Graham in the *Daily Mirror* in July of 1958. The critics agreed. *The Bravados* was the story of a manhunt, with Gregory Peck playing a man whose wife and child have been murdered and who is searching for the killers. Joan was cast as the romantic interest, and *The New York Times* said she was 'pretty but not really necessary'. She was a distraction from the 'find 'em and shoot 'em' tone of the movie.

Being miscast, in unsuitable roles, had become Joan's calling card – in movies as well as in her personal life.

In August of 1984 Cloris Leachman was a guest on NBC-TV's *The Johnny Carson Show*. Guest hostess Joan Rivers asked Cloris about Joan Collins's affair with George Englund. Leachman recalled a phone call she had gotten from Joan during this period in which Joan declared her love for George, acknowledging Cloris's love for him as well. 'I found myself spouting all this "B" dialogue,' Leachman said, and the assessment seems accurate. Brought up on Hollywood movies and a victim of her own press in the fan magazines, Joan's way of dealing with life was as close as one could get to a 'B' movie without actually having cameras running. With any luck, and a good deal of maturation, this would change. But the change was still some time away in 1959 and 1960.

6

Out of the Contract and into the Chopped Liver

By 1959 Joan was earning $80,000 a year. 'I appeared in nothing but flops,' she said recently. 'But I can hardly blame anyone. I was so young and inexperienced, both in acting and in life.' Still, it wasn't a bad salary for someone with so little experience.

But money, as we know, isn't everything, and Joan was a woman who was looking for everything. She was currently working on *Seven Thieves*, in which she played a stripper, and was taking lessons from Candy Barr. Candy was 'the favorite stripteaser of the Sunset Strip', as Sidney Skolsky called her in his *New York Post* column devoted to Joan and Candy on August 11, 1959. Candy taught her that 'the less you reveal, the more exciting it is'. Joan later said: 'I have to say that I became a pretty expert stripper.' The reviews agreed. When the movie came out, Joan was praised, even if most of the critics felt that the script and directing lacked energy. The energy Joan was exhibiting may have come from the fact that she was happy. She had found another 'everything'. His name was Warren Beatty.

Feeling trod upon by George (who was still making and breaking promises to leave Cloris) and feeling badly about the fact that the lead in *Cleopatra* would probably go to someone else, Joan discovered Warren Beatty. He was sitting across from her in a restaurant one August evening. She was with friends and he was with a young starlet named Jane Fonda. In 1959 Jane Fonda was still known in Hollywood as 'Henry Fonda's daughter' and Beatty was known as 'Shirley MacLaine's kid brother'. 'I felt this myopic, pimply faced boy across the room staring at me,' Joan has since said. Still, she found *something* attractive enough about Shirley's twenty-two-year-old brother to stare back, however briefly. She was still leading a double life, dating other men as cover-ups while she waited for George to get his act together, and she was constantly feuding with Fox, which continued to offer her lousy roles. At this point there was nowhere for her to go but up.

The flirtation with Beatty went nowhere that evening. A few weeks later Joan went to a party at a friend's, and Warren was there, playing the piano – brilliantly. They didn't speak that evening either, but apparently something was happening. The following day Warren called Joan six times, having gotten her number from friends. A woman as beautiful as Joan is hard to miss, and Warren didn't miss her. He finally reached her (instead of her answering service) and asked her to dinner. She accepted.

Over a Mexican dinner she found him irresistible, charming, and easy to talk to. His birthday, furthermore, was March 30, only one day earlier than Sydney Chaplin's. Joan was always attracted to Aries men, and since she was, and is, a staunch believer in astrology, she took this as a good omen. (Max Reed had been an Aries as well, but one of the nice things about astrology is that you can like it when you want to and ignore it at other times.) When it came time for her and Warren to part for the evening, they didn't.

They saw each other constantly. He was, she told a friend, sexually the best thing that had ever happened to her. Her astrologer had told her that 'Aries men are ruled by their cocks', and in Warren's case it seemed to be true. They made love three, four, five times a day. He was 'insatiable', and she was in heaven. She had admitted that it eventually wore her out and made fer feel like a 'sex object', but for the moment it was grand, just what the doctor ordered.

Joan got her courage up and sent George a 'dear John' telegram in the Orient (one of his all too frequent trips). It was abrupt and to the point, explaining to him that she had fallen in love with someone else. When he returned, he called and they met for a drink; she felt she owed him that much courtesy. As always, he was charming and believable. He told her that Warren was a boy and that what she needed was a man. He still loved her. He begged her to think it over for a week. The one-hour meeting that had begun with Joan feeling that she was, in her own words, 'about to get rid of Daddy', ended with her wondering if she could possibly be in love with two men at the same time.

Warren was furious that she had even gone to see George, and jealous of the attention she was lavishing on her ex-lover. The following day he followed her to the set of *Seven Thieves* and pleaded his case to her. She was unhappy and confused and agreed to talk it over with her psychiatrist at her next session. The session was a tough one: *Should I or shouldn't I; is it worth it; is it part of my father fixation; do I deserve to be happy?* She finally made the decision to drop George; he was genuinely not doing her any good. When they next saw each other, she told him that she loved him but that he would never make her happy and that *she deserved to be happy*. They parted friends. To the naked eye it looked as if Joan had taken a giant step toward growing up.

Warren, however, was possessive and reportedly tried to run her career. She had been offered a part in Fox's upcoming version of D. H. Lawrence's *Sons and Lovers*, but she hated the script. It was the third script in two years she had turned down from Fox and they were getting more than a little angry. She read the revised script but still was not happy. In addition, and probably more important, making the film would have meant having to go to England, and Warren was presently doing theatre work in the States. He begged her not to take the part, not to leave him. She agreed. Years later Joan told her daughter: 'Don't give your life over to a man. Don't put your personal life in front of your career.' This advice, this realization, however, was twenty years away, and Joan had to learn it for herself.

When she failed to show up on the set of *Sons and Lovers*, she was suspended without salary for eight weeks – a $16,000 loss. She told Hedda Hopper that she found the role of a 'nymphomaniac suffragette' repugnant and was sick of being cast as a sexpot. 'I think doing stupid parts in stupid pictures can destroy a career,' Hopper quoted her in the *Los Angeles Times*. She wanted to be released from her contract, but Fox made her promise to do two more pictures. The decision not to do *Sons and Lovers* turned out to be wrong. It was 'infinitely better' than most of her movies, Joan admitted later, but being in love with Warren and wanting to make him happy helped sway her in the direction of the wrong decision.

'I should have been born three hundred years ago,' Joan told Irene Thirer in the *New York Post* in February of 1960. 'I'm a completely old-fashioned girl. I don't think females are equal to males. Man is superior, stronger physically, more intellectual, more logical. And I'm jolly glad!' She continued in this vein, finally arriving at 'I don't want to be independent and make decisions. Unfortunately, I am, and I do!' Changing her philosophy with the whims of the men with whom she was involved was par for the course.

Hollywood loved the new couple. They spelled 'romance' to all their fans. In a wonderful yellow-journalistic piece in the April issue of *Photoplay*, writer George Christy helped his readers 'relive' the earliest moments of Joan's relationship with Warren. Beginning with a fictionalized conversation Joan was presumed to be having with herself before she met Warren, the piece, called 'Nothing Matters when You're in Love', contains the following 'inner feelings':

> She'd just returned from another evening of watching television with friends. 'You're ... you're unhappy,' something inside her seemed to insist, 'because you've made a mess of your personal life. You made a mess of one marriage and you've been trying to make up for it ever since ... And all you've managed to prove is that you're getting nowhere fast. You run to parties and good times, dating millionaire actors and handsome princes [a wonderfully veiled reference to Trujillo] – but have they made you happy?'

In this piece she meets Warren (as it happened), and he asks her out (as it happened). The article takes them through their dinner. Joan looks into his 'blue eyes that were mysterious and deep', and they confide secret things to each other, like the fact that he was so nervous before their date that he went out and had an ice cream cone, and that she had 'changed since [she] met [him]', i.e., she used to go to large well-known restaurants.

Joan is quoted as saying that because he always lit her cigarettes, opened doors for her, and stood up when she came into a room, he made her feel like a lady. Later on in the relationship she 'wanted him to be a success'.

> Certainly he's trying to get ahead, to find some security. He doesn't take me to smart places. He can't afford them. But all these things don't matter, somehow. Nothing matters when you're in love except your deep-rooted belief in each other.

The glorious thing about this fictionalized account is that it is precisely the way Joan looked at it. She was always a hopeless romantic, and this was just the sort of love affair she was looking for. Needless to say, it delighted their fans, who realized that a movie star could be as dewy-eyed as they were, and still be famous and glamorous. Warren and Joan referred to each other as 'butterfly' and 'bee'. It was more than the fans had ever dreamed of, and the fact that it was only the 'up' side of the relationship made it even better.

The couple settled into a small apartment in Los Angeles. Their sex life continued nonstop ('an oyster in a slot machine', Joan later said, rather unromantically) and they were content. Warren's ambition was almost as overwhelming as his libido (even this is suggested in the *Photoplay* article), and he was working hard at getting the lead in *Splendor in the Grass*. Joan was back on salary (she was supporting the two of them, so the money was urgently needed) and was planning to make *Big River, Big Man*. (She never did, as it turns out.) Things were going well. Then Joan discovered she was pregnant.

Tormented, frightened, and confused, they discussed the possibilities. They ruled out immediate marriage and having the baby. Abortion was their only recourse. At this point in time, abortion was illegal everywhere in the United States, and Joan and Warren found themselves in a very difficult situation. 'Doctors' in Mexico were known to perform abortions, but Joan was not about to take her life in her hands by going to one of them. Through a connection of Warren's they found an abortionist in New Jersey. Utterly terrified, with recurrent nightmares about Max Reed coming to cut her up, Joan kept vacillating; sometimes she wanted the baby, often she knew it would be crazy to have it, she wondered whether Warren was right for her, she suspected she might be a bad mother. She was afraid. 'Having a baby will wreck both of our careers,' Warren explained, and Joan gave in.

After the abortion they took an apartment in New York. Warren got the lead in *Splendor in the Grass* and Joan was studying for what turned out to be her last film for Fox, another Biblical epic called *Esther and the King*. Joan was about to embark for Rome to begin filming when Warren presented her with an engagement ring that he had hidden in a container of chopped liver. 'Are you sure you really want to – I mean you're not just doing this to make me feel secure, are you?' Joan asked, her sixth sense working overtime. No, he assured her weakly, he meant it. Somewhere in the back of her mind at all times were the warnings her best friend and her astrologer had given her: *Warren is very ambitious; he has a great deal of growing up to do; you won't marry him.*

She left for Rome but flew back a few days later just to be with him. The gossip columnists loved it. Considering the way the film turned out, she should have stayed in New York. *The New York Times* referred to it as a 'sluggish, horse-operatic pretense', and Joan, herself, later told the New York *World Telegram* that 'it was dreadful. I hope nobody saw it.' She sensed it was a mess before the critics saw it and knew that it would be the box office catastrophe it turned out to be. Her career was at a new low; she might as well marry Warren.

During the filming she came back to see Warren in New York again. They fought constantly. He accused her of being unfaithful to him and she wondered if the pot wasn't calling the kettle black. She returned to Rome angry. Again she flew back to New York in the middle of filming. She hated *Esther and the King* but her real reason for her current transoceanic trips was to make certain that she didn't lose another man. The old pattern was setting in: She didn't really want Warren, but she was afraid of losing him. He called her and sent her notes daily, but when they were together, they fought. Her wedding dress was almost ready and the tabloids were full of items about the engaged couple. It was a real marriage made

Joan Collins has always been a beauty. As an aspiring actress, she found her first success modelling for covers of 'true crime' magazines. (*Museum of Modern Art/Film Stills Archive*)

Joan's earliest films were for the most part entirely forgettable potboilers and exploitation quickies. Her first big break came when she was cast as the sultry Princess Nellifer in the epic *Land of the Pharaohs*. (*Modern Screen Archives*)

Some of Joan's early film roles were not exactly cast to type. Here she is dressed as a nun for *Sea Wife*, in which she costarred with a young Richard Burton. (*Museum of Modern Art/Film Stills Archive*)

In the midst of playing Hollywood starlet Joan had to face a real-life crisis when husband Maxwell Reed sued for divorce and demanded alimony. Her sister Jackie supported her during the court proceedings. (*Museum of Modern Art/Film Stills Archive*)

Meanwhile, the publicity mills continued to generate stories aimed at cleaning up Joan's image. Here she and George Nader receive awards from *Photoplay* magazine naming them among 'the most promising'. (*Museum of Modern Art/Film Stills Archive*)

Joan Collins taking it easy in her Hollywood apartment.

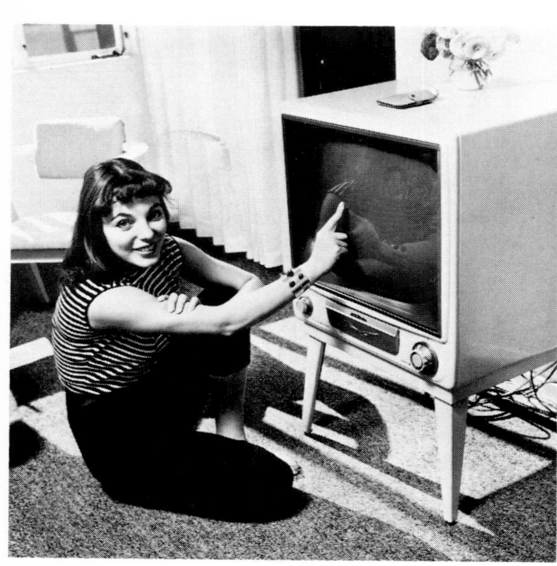

(Photos on these pages credited to the Museum of Modern Art/Film Stills Archive)

Boyfriend Sidney Chaplin played an important role in Joan's life, teaching her the value of laughter. He was a great source of comfort to her when her marriage to Max Reed hit the skids. (*AP/Wide World Photos*)

Another boyfriend and frequent Hollywood escort was the young Arthur Loew. A wedding with him, however, was not in Joan's future. (*Museum of Modern Art/Film Stills Archive*)

Meanwhile, Joan continued to appear in movies. Here Joan embraces Stephen Boyd in *Island in the Sun*. (*Modern Screen Archives*)

Joan was ravishing in her biopic portrayal of Evelyn Nesbit in *The Girl in the Red Velvet Swing*. Here she is seen with Miss Nesbit and costar Farley Granger. (*Museum of Modern Art/Film Stills Archive*)

It was in a musical remake of *The Women*, entitled *The Opposite Sex*, that Joan first played the catty, superbitch character that was later to become her stock-in-trade in the *Dynasty* TV series. A similar though more comic part followed in *Rally 'Round the Flag, Boys*. (*Museum of Modern Art/Film Stills Archive*)

Still there were the obligatory publicity shots for the fan mags to contend with. Some of them were less inane than others. (*Museum of Modern Art/Film Stills Archive*)

in Hollywood and the fan magazines went crazy. Everyone was looking forward to the wedding, it seemed. Everyone except the bride and groom.

Time passed and the relationship became more and more fragile. Joan was released from her Fox contract and spent time reading new scripts from other companies. Warren hated them all and tossed them out. Joan was being practical and trying to find work so she could continue to live well. Warren still wasn't helping out much with the finances, so he could afford to make more artistically based career decisions. Joan, always the survivor, just needed work.

Warren was going to London to begin work on *The Roman Spring of Mrs Stone*, and since Joan's mother had become ill and her sister, Jackie, had gotten married, Joan went along. It was a good way of seeing the family and at the same time keeping an eye on Warren. She and Warren fought with each other while they were there and Joan moved back in with her mother. She wasn't looking forward to getting married, and despite the fact that her mother thought Warren was wonderful, she too agreed that Warren wasn't a very good gamble.

When Joan and Warren returned to Los Angeles, Joan's mother and brother came to visit. Warren made it clear how little he liked having them there and Joan was horrified at his selfishness. Filled with the usual self-doubts, after a two-year engagement (longer than most Hollywood marriages), she decided to end it. She was offered a role Warren thought was 'crap', and she decided to take it. Warren asked why. 'Two reasons,' she said. 'For the money – and to get away from you.'

Years later Joan said about Warren Beatty: 'When I knew him, he was certainly running after the people who could be of benefit to him in his career. Bloody clever.' At the time, her closest friend had told Joan that he was probably using her 'to get ahead'. All the facts, all the evidence, seem to have been there. 'Or was it,' Joan wondered at the time, 'that I only wanted the neurotic ones, the men unable truly to love – truly to support and truly to give. Only by gaining the love of one of these impossible men could I prove to myself that I was a worthy person.'

Two questions stand out. Would this need ever be filled? Would Joan ever change?

7
Home Again, Home Again

In August of 1961 Joan was again living in London and had just landed the female lead in *Road to Hong Kong* (the script Warren had referred to as 'crap') opposite Bob Hope and Bing Crosby. She was free of Twentieth Century-Fox and had gotten the role on her own. In an article called 'Joan Collins Went Out and Got Herself a Job', published in the New York *World Telegram* in April of 1962, Joan describes her new philosophy: 'A girl has to look out for herself these days if she wants to survive in the movies. I was in London when I heard that Norman Panama and Melvin Frank were going to make *Road to Hong Kong* with Bob Hope and Bing Crosby there and they were looking for a leading lady. So I offered my services. They liked me and I got the part.' At the end of the interview Joan says, 'I'm looking out for myself.' And indeed it is obvious that she was looking out for herself, because there was no one else to look out for her – she was independent of a man and a studio affiliation; she was out there alone.

Road to Hong Kong was a comedy and Joan knew her affinity for comedy. 'When a girl knows what she wants, she should go after it,' she told Bob Thomas in the New York *Daily Mirror* from London in August. 'I won't see the London press anymore,' she added. 'They hate me and I don't care. I think I'll marry an American and become a citizen.' She was referring, of course, to Warren, to whom she was still engaged when she gave this interview. In October of 1961, two months later, Hyman Goldberg reported in the same newspaper the news of their breakup, accompanied by the news that Joan was dating Robert Wagner and Warren was dating Wagner's ex-wife, Natalie Wood. Joan had never liked Natalie – she found her incredibly vain – and a few years before, when Natalie and Bob had announced their plans to marry, Joan was overheard to say 'He'll need all the luck in the world with that dame.' She therefore must have been slightly pleased that Warren and Natalie had somehow wound up together.

At least in part convinced that Warren's interest in Natalie was due to his ambition – he liked being seen with 'major stars' – Joan was glad to be rid of him. She and Wagner had been very good friends since they worked together on *Stopover Tokyo*. The press was reporting that their involvement was romantic, but Joan denied it. Wagner wasn't her type. 'I was still neurotic enough to only be truly interested in complex, difficult men,' she wrote later, 'and R.J. [her nickname for Wagner] was gentle and sweet and too nice for me to become involved with.' Well, at least she was aware of her problems, even if there was nothing she could do about them.

Three things kept her busy in London. One was making the *Road* movie, another was the serious illness of her mother, and the last, and, as it turns out, most important, was her burgeoning love affair with Anthony Newley.

The filming went well. Joan was an adept comedienne and her role as a sexy spy suited her well. The reviews for this final *Road* picture (there had been six previously) were kind to Joan, and no one seemed to mind that Joan had a better part than Dorothy Lamour. Lamour was in the picture. But along with the comedy on the screen came tragedy in Joan's life.

Her mother, whom she had adored and felt sorry for, was

dying. A few days before her death, with Joan at her bedside. Elsa Collins confronted her. In her weakened state, and without Joe standing there to criticize and judge her harshly, she asked Joan what she was planning to do with the rest of her life. She told her it was time for her to settle down, and she hoped Joan would have children. Elsa Collins had lived for her children and it was the only way she knew how to be happy and she wanted the same thing for Joan. Jackie had recently given birth to a daughter and seemed wonderfully happy. Joan and Elsa felt closer than they had ever felt before. When Elsa died a few days later, Joan made a promise to herself to do what would have made her mother happy. 'I had an ambition and a goal now. For her. And I was going to make it happen ... come what may.' Fortunately, Joan had a man in mind.

Anthony Newley was the rage of London. He was starring in his own show, *Stop the World – I Want to Get Off*. The critics had damned it as self-indulgent, but it was an enormously popular success. It was a show in which Newley could, and did, perform nonstop, exhibiting all the highs and lows of a human being's life. It was sort of a theatrical nervous breakdown and it moved audiences to tears. The show's hit tune was 'What Kind of Fool Am I?' in which the central character proclaims his inability to love. Bob Wagner got a pair of tickets to the show and invited Joan. She had spotted Newley in a restaurant a few weeks before and had recognized him from his child-actor days. She was interested in what this 'genius', as he was being called, was up to now.

She was knocked out by the show, 'mesmerized', as she put it. Newley reminded her of Charlie Chaplin and she found him 'spectacularly talented'. She and R.J. went backstage and lavished praise on Newley. The three went off to a quiet dinner and Joan felt comfortable and happy. 'There's a certain fun that Brits have with one another,' she explained later.

She hadn't had that fun in Hollywood; although she had adapted well to the States, she was still at heart a Brit. She felt at home, somehow, with Newley. She had also just broken up with Beatty and was feeling needy. A few days later a mutual friend confided that Newley was very interested in her. He was married but 'informally separated', and the friend told Joan that he had never really been in love – much, if not exactly, like the character in his play.

'How sad – how challenging,' Joan thought, making emotional preparations to leap, as usual, into the void. 'Any woman with any horse sense does not fall in love with a man who openly proclaims to the world in song and verse that he is unable to love. . . . If she is smart and clever she will not get involved.' If, one might add, she is smart and clever but likes trouble, she will. And Joan did.

Newley had an eye for the ladies – Joan knew that. He was moody and hypochondriacal. He was a Libra, absolutely unsuited for Gemini Joan. They went out for three weeks before they went to bed together, and when they did, it was hardly the romantic scene Joan or her fans would have liked. She was at home at her parents' house, sick in bed with the flu. Newley dropped by and made love to her then and there, amidst used Kleenex and cough medicine. He left in a wonderful mood; Joan felt singularly unexcited. A few days later she discovered that he was at that time involved with a young starlet. While she found this bothersome, she was already hooked. He was so wrong, he had to be right.

They dated for months, and she became the perfect wife, albeit an unmarried one. She devoted her days and nights to him. He was accustomed to being taken care of and she rose to the occasion. His mother came to his flat every morning to make him breakfast, so Joan would have to do better than that. She turned down movie offers (shades of Warren Beatty) in order to be with him. He continued to flirt around. Furthermore, Joan has written that his tastes ran to young girls but Joan tried to convince herself that this tendency would pass, once they got married and had children. Her self-delusory apparatus was working at full tilt.

Joan became close friends with Leslie Bricusse, Tony's collaborator on *Stop the World*, and with his wife, Evie. After her mother's death Joan returned to Los Angeles, and Tony, Leslie, and Evie came to visit. They had a wonderful, carefree time and Joan decided that she was definitely going to marry Tony. She loved him and wanted to be with him. She wanted children; she needed children. Besides, her career was at a virtual standstill. Tony was almost divorced.

After their vacation Tony returned to London for a few months and then came back to the States to ready *Stop the World* for American audiences. The couple met in Philadelphia, where the show was having a tryout. But Joan left him, vowing not to get involved, when, as she recalls, Tony confessed to an affair he had been having with a sixteen-year-old girl. Joan had learned. Their engagement, informal though it was, was broken.

Joan went to New York for a little rest and to await the opening of Tony's play. *Stop the World* opened to unbelievably bad notices, but word-of-mouth was spectacular and it sold out for a long run instantly. Stinging from Tony's inability to either commit himself or to remain faithful, Joan began a brief fling with the young British actor Terence Stamp, who happened to be in New York (and staying at Joan's hotel) at the same time. Newley fumed and sent friends to plead his case to Joan. He wanted her back. She did her best to remain firm in her resolve, but eventually gave in when he promised to try to keep away from young girls. They set up house in New York.

Soon after, Tony's divorce became final and they were married.

It had been eleven years between marriages for Joan. She had often said that she would wait until she was mature enough to marry again, and she had. On October 12, 1963, Joan fulfilled her silent promise to her mother.

'You don't know why Tony missed the matinee of *Stop the World* on October 11, 1963,' Joan told the *Sunday News* in May 1965. 'Well, I can tell you. We didn't enter into our marriage lightly. We wanted the facts of life. And at two minutes before 2 P.M. that afternoon I gave birth to Tara by natural childbirth. It was part of our agreement,' she continued, 'and our desire and our need that Tony be there as fathers should be, for the delivery of the child.'

It looked as if the three Newleys – Joan, Tony, and newborn Tara – were going to take root in New York. Joan had practically become a Tony and Tara groupie. For now, her career was the last thing on her mind. She breast-fed Tara and watched the child's daily growth. If she had ever been in love in her life, it was with her daughter, 'the most beautiful creature' she had ever seen. Tara bloomed. *Stop the World* was scheduled to close in December and Tony was itching to get back to England, where he felt he belonged and where he was more comfortable. They uprooted after a year in New York and left for Europe.

They went to Paris, where they intended to stay for a few months before they could return to England owing to Tony's tax situation (the end of the tax year in Great Britain is April). Joan took well to being a mother while Tony wrote. It wasn't easy being married to a 'work-driven genius', Joan later said, but for the moment, and maybe for the first time in her life, Joan was happy.

'One early morning,' the New York *Herald Tribune* reported in March of 1964, 'the Newleys were awakened by an uproar ... opened the door and found the corridor awash in smoke and flame. [Their hotel] had caught fire ... "It was like a horrible nightmare" said Joan. "I really thought my life was going to end."' The whole experience, and Joan's terrible fears for herself, Tony, and Tara, gave Joan such bad dreams that they packed their bags and left for Switzerland.

They stayed at the very posh Palace Hotel in St Moritz, which was owned by the husband of Joan's best friend. All the other mothers in the international jet set who frequented the Palace found Joan the most unlikely person ever to have dropped in. Not only did she take care of her own child (the other mothers had nannies for theirs), she dressed down and preferred to spend time with her child and husband. Tony hated 'society' crowds anyway, and Joan was just as pleased. They spent a month in St Moritz and then left for London.

They settled down again. Joan was pregnant once more and Tony was obsessed with his work. Tara was happy and thriving. The Newleys socialized with the Bricusses. Joan lost the baby she was carrying and took her agent up on an offer to make an Italian comedy in Rome. The film, *La Conguintura*, was never released in either Great Britain or the United States, but Joan loved making it and it was a great success in Italy. Mother and daughter enjoyed being on location and Tony kept busy at home with readying his new play, *The Roar of the Greasepaint, the Smell of the Crowd*, to open in the West End. The reviews were even less generous for this one than they had been for *Stop the World*, but again producer David Merrick picked the play up for Broadway. And once again, the Newleys moved to New York.

This time they rented an elegant town house in the east 60s and played host and hostess to Tony's parents, Joan's sister, Jackie, and Jackie's daughter. In January of 1965 Joan told Leonard Harris in the New York *World Telegram* that she 'couldn't care less' if she ever made another movie. She explained that she was lazy, she was happy taking care of her baby, and she couldn't see herself doing the things an actress has to do to promote herself. In addition, she had hated being bullied by Fox. '"Don't muss your hair, Joan." "Turn your head, Joan, that's not your good side." "Don't smile too much, Joan, you'll show your gums."' She was content being away from all that. All she wanted was a place of her own to live in, and she wasn't looking forward to the fourteen weeks they were about to spend on the road with *The Roar of the Greasepaint.*

When they returned from their travels, they rented a furnished apartment and moved their eighty pieces of luggage into it. Most of their belongings were either in storage or at friends' houses and Joan was pregnant again. The new play opened in May, and on May 23, the New York *Daily News* ran a lengthy piece called 'The Wonderful World of Anthony Newley'. In the article, which happened to have been published on Joan's birthday (they erroneously reported it to be her thirtieth birthday; it was actually her thirty-second), much of the copy was given over to her. She seemed to be an ecstatically happy woman; Tony had been at the birth of their first child, 'as fathers should be', and the article stressed the fact that Joan was no longer the 'playgirl of the western world'.

'I just hope I won't be so unbearable to live with now that the show is on,' Tony said, implying great self-awareness and concern. 'Joan has been so sympathetic through it all.' This turns out to have been an understatement; Joan had entirely tucked away her career in order to be Tony's wife and Tara's mother.

There were problems, however. Joan was feeling rootless; all this shuttling from one place to another was reminding her of the London Blitz, when the family moved every few weeks to avoid the bombing. During the summer, in the last two months of her pregnancy, the Newleys rented a house on

Sands Point, Long Island, and Joan was interviewed in the 'At home with ...' column in the *New York Post*. She said that she regretted that Tara had never had a nursery of her own and that they had no real home except for a house in England in which they had never even spent one night! The interviewer, trying desperately to get an angle on Joan Collins, happy homemaker, asked Joan about a big barbecue they had recently held for the cast of Tony's play. 'Everybody asked me what kind [of dressing] was on the salad, and I showed them the bottle – Kraft's French,' Joan told her. Some things, it seems, never change.

The Newleys' son, Sacha (Alexander Anthony) was born in New York on September 8, 1965. Within a few weeks Joan knew what the term 'sibling rivalry' meant. Tara was wildly jealous of her younger brother and she nearly drove Joan crazy. One would have thought that Joan would sympathize with Tara – hadn't she been displaced by Jackie?

Within a few months Tony decided that the future for his career was in movies, and the couple again uprooted, this time heading for California. Joan was just as pleased. She suspected that Tony was sleeping with other women in New York and she was glad to get away.

Back in Los Angeles Joan began feeling like a has-been, like Tony Newley's wife, and little more. She wasn't used to it. Her social life was limited and her career was of little interest to anyone but herself. In June of 1966 Tony and Joan played host and hostess at Jackie's second marriage (to businessman Oscar Lerman). The London *Evening Standard* reported the marriage of twenty-six-year-old (years tended to melt off Jackie's age even more than they did off Joan's) Jackie and added: 'And last night she telephoned her father, Mr Joe Collins, in London to say: "I'm getting married in the morning."' Jackie's reverence with regard to her father was yet another difference between the Collins girls.

Joan did a guest spot in a movie called *Warning Shot* (other guest stars were Lillian Gish and Carroll O'Connor), but that wasn't enough to keep her busy. Television was the direction in which everyone was going and Joan needed the work and the diversion. It had been nine years since she had told *Photoplay* that television was 'the ultimate in boredom', but people and styles change. Joan, always the survivor, was more than willing to make the change. Because she was convinced that Tony could not remain faithful, her marriage was crumbling. Joan was a lucky woman in some ways, since when her career faltered she turned to men, and vice versa. She had two interests that took up her time (besides her children) and she could always call on one of them. Tony was very busy making *Dr Dolittle* and Joan made appearances in the television shows *Run for Your Life* and *The Man from U.N.C.L.E.* At the same time, she decided to enjoy a dalliance with Ryan O'Neal, partially in exchange for the extracurricular activities Tony was involved in.

'I've always been good at discovering talent,' Joan told an interviewer a couple of years ago with regard to her affair with Ryan O'Neal. They met at a fashionable disco in Beverly Hills. He asked her to dance; she thought he was gorgeous. The jukebox was playing 'I Can't Get No Satisfaction' and it reminded her of her marriage. He was sexy and straightforward, quite a change from Tony, who, Joan recalls, said 'thank you' after sex and retreated into his dark moods half the time. Joan was opposed to extramarital affairs, however, and let O'Neal's interest go unsatisfied.

She did a guest stint on *Star Trek* (which has become a classic – one of the best and most legendary shows on that most popular of series) and worried about her marriage. She wondered how, if ever, she would solve its problems. One evening when Tony was feeling too tired to go out, she went to a party with friends. They wound up, late in the evening, at the same disco as before, and Ryan was there again. They danced until late and he made very heavy and obvious advances. Then he drove her home. She refused to go to his place despite his pleas, but she did promise to call him. She knew it was trouble, and she did her best to avoid it. It was a new kind of trouble for her – one she didn't need and had no rules for. But it also looked like fun. A while later Ryan showed up on the set where she was taping *Run for Your Life* and took her to lunch. It was May 22, the day before her birthday, and Tony had just called from New York to say that he wouldn't be back in time to celebrate with her. 'I decided what I wanted for my birthday present. A girl should get the best she deserves on her birthday. And he was.' Thus does Joan describe the start of her affair with Ryan O'Neal. Love never really entered into her affair with O'Neal – she reports that he was imaginative and inventive and fun to be with. He had two children and was divorced. Tony went to London to finish work on *Dr Dolittle* and Joan worked on a *Batman* episode for ABC-TV and *The Virginian* for NBC. She and Ryan were seen often together, and the tabloids got wind of their affair.

Joan was sick of herself for not being able to end her pathetic marriage. She saw Newley as yet another in a long line of men 'who used women on their climb up the ladder, who basically hated the whole bloody female sex'. She was still trying for Daddy. She had gone back into analysis, but actually already had the answers. She wanted to find the world's most difficult man and have him love her totally. It was a completely self-destructive mode of behavior, but it was like having blue eyes or fair skin. She was stuck with it. It was in her genes.

8

Polyester Poontang, Happy at Last

Being considered a star seems to come from within. It is a matter of attitude that changes starlets into stars, and Joan's change in attitude seems to have come when she left Fox. Starlets' professional lives are controlled by others; stars control their own. By 1962 Joan was searching for properties for herself and was planning to set up her own production company, Harley Productions, named for the street her parents lived on in London. Furthermore, starlets, like their fans, believe what they see in the movies and read in the tabloids. But by May of 1962 Joan's attitude toward that had changed as well. She told Sheila Graham in the London *Courier Journal* that she had been 'weaned on movies. Everything in the movies is simply lovely. Only in time do you know that no one is perfect and only then can you love people for their faults.' Her relationship with Anthony Newley, despite this newfound wisdom, was a giant step backward. In essence, he turned her back into a starlet, at least for a while.

In December of 1967 *Time* magazine sported a picture of the Newleys at the Manhattan opening of *Dr Dolittle*. The couple looked radiant, and far happier than they were. All eyes were on her dress. 'I'm not an exhibitionist,' Joan told the press. Tony made no comment at all about whether or not *he* was an exhibitionist, but his next film answered the question. It also gave pause to the wisdom of not believing what one sees in the movies.

Can Hieronymus Merkin Ever Forget Mercy Humppe and Find True Happiness? was yet another chapter in the long-winded continuing autobiography Tony was turning out, and it was by far the worst to date. The natives on Malta, where the work was filmed, demonstrated against Newley, his cast, and crew for making 'a dirty picture on their lovely, clean island', as Newley put it in the *New York Daily News* on March 16, 1969.

The film concerns a man, nude a good deal of the time, who is torn between having affairs with every young pretty thing that comes along and remaining with Polyester Poontang, the mother of his two children. Joan was cast as Polyester, and Sacha and Tara appeared as the fictional(?) couple's children. *Playboy* centerfold Connie Kreski played Mercy Humppe, who turns out to be the love of the Merkin/Newley character's life. Joan wanted the part of the wife despite the fact that it reflected her own marriage role; perhaps she was 'working through', as the psychoanalytical expression goes. The New York *Morning Telegraph* called it a 'pointless, witless, sniggering obscenity'. *The New York Times* wasn't as kind: 'Newley so overextends and overexposes himself that the movie comes to look like an act of professional suicide.' Suicide or not, the blatant admission of infidelity and the obvious subservient role into which producer, director, writer, and star Newley had placed his wife effectively plunged a dagger into the heart of their marriage. Newley, through the film, heaped more abuse on Joan than she had suffered in any of her starlet parts. It opened the unhappiness of her private life to the public in a manner so hideous and insulting that she was left with little choice.

The Newleys were living in London temporarily. Tony was

finishing up the editing and cutting of his new epic and Joan was living in torment, trying to find a way out of their marriage that would not hurt the children. During this period she made a film called *Subterfuge*, a mediocre spy drama. *Variety* said that the film 'showcases Joan Collins's special physical attractiveness', but was poorly made. 'In course of story development Miss Collins's young son is kidnapped,' the review continues. 'While the actress appears properly distraught in scene in which she is informed of this fact, two scenes and some hours later she appears in highest of high fashion clothes and complicated new hairstyle. Ridiculous effect of scene is to make it appear the worried mom had spent the afternoon at Harrods and at the hairdresser to impress some thugs.'

It is easier to understand why Joan Collins, the woman, would look distraught at this juncture in her life, and one can also understand why she would want to look her best. She hated her marriage and had met the man she 'had been searching for all of her life'.

Ron Kass was the managing director of Apple Records, the Beatles' record company. Joan and Tony, some friends, and the recently separated-from-his-wife Ron Kass had dinner together one evening at one of the more fashionable restaurant-discos in London. (Joan almost always met the men she was to fall in love with in restaurants, for whatever that's worth.) Tony noticed Joan and Ron's attraction to each other, but knowing that his marriage was on the rocks anyway, and preferring work to play, he excused himself and left. When Joan realized how strong, sensitive, and loving Ron was, she was fascinated. When she discovered that his birthday was March 30, the same as Sydney Chaplin's and Warren Beatty's, she was hooked.

Because Tony worked all the time, and because the Newleys had come to terms with their wrecked marriage and had an arrangement that they would lead relatively separate lives but remain somewhat together (mostly for the children), Joan was able to see a great deal of Ron. She had never had any trouble getting a man she was interested in when she was a starlet, and as a thirty-six-year-old woman, a star, she had even less. She had lost none of her glamor; the *Variety* review of *Can Hieronymus Merkin Ever Forget Mercy Humppe and Find True Happiness?* said 'Miss Collins is even more beautiful than when she was under contract to Twentieth Century-Fox in the 1950s.' Joan was getting better with age. She and Ron took their time before they plunged headlong into an affair, but once they did, there was no turning back.

They were separated from each other while Joan did a cameo in *If It's Tuesday This Must Be Belgium*, and for a longer time when she went to Italy to make an artsy Italian film that was called *State of Siege* (not to be confused with the 1973 Costa-Gavras film). In the latter Joan did her first nude scene, opposite young Mathieu Carrière. She reports that she was frightened by the prospect of her nude scene (my, how people change!), but enjoyed the role of a 'desolate young widow who becomes involved in a love affair with a seventeen-year-old boy'. With Tony's record company in London Joan recorded an album of songs, which was to be called *And She Sings Too!*, and the couple found themselves working very closely together at the most distant point in their marriage.

The Newleys returned to Hollywood after Joan made a film called *The Executioner* with George Peppard. It was a spy drama and made a good impression generally; Joan was seen only as 'neatly ornamental' in the film by *The New York Times*, but at least she was working.

Ron Kass was living in Hollywood as well and their affair continued. When he went to Rio de Janeiro on business, Joan realized that she couldn't keep the affair going without some sort of commitment on both sides. She called him in Rio and they spoke for an hour. By the end of the conversation Joan decided that she would get a divorce. She and Ron would marry.

The divorce came through seven years after the marriage began (something else her astrologist had told her), and they tried to make it as amicable as possible. Tony turned against Joan in the media, however, and it hurt her feelings and her pride. He said, on a TV talk show, 'I work for an organization that supports Joan Collins. I keep [her] in the style to which she became accustomed during her marriage to me.' He was referring to their divorce settlement and the child support he was paying her, but Joan is quick to point out that she was earning her own money as well, and was not relying wholly on Tony. One might also point out that during their marriage Joan's movie career was at a standstill, in part at least, because she was devoting herself to Tony and the children. A woman who was earning $80,000 a year in the late fifties can hardly be considered a freeloader, and the fact that she had chosen to *stop* earning that sort of money to take care of her family says more for her than Tony's accusations can take away.

She next made *Up in the Cellar*, 'a tasteless, dull piece of idiocy', as *The New York Times* called it. Joan played the 'pin-headed, astrology-minded' wife of a college president who is seduced by a student who has gone crazy. It is interesting only because Joan's co-star (and on-screen husband) was Larry Hagman, the man who now plays J.R. Ewing on *Dallas*. J.R. and Alexis are currently the two most beloved villains on television, but apparently their energies were misspent in this film.

She and Ron moved back to London but lived separately, mostly so as not to confuse or disturb Tara and Sacha. Ron wanted to marry, but Joan was feeling gun-shy, even if deeply in love. Needing money, wanting to survive as a star, woman, and mother, Joan threw herself into making a series of quick horror movies.

Quest for Love was a science fiction film about a man who finds himself in a parallel dimension and sees the counterparts of his life. (If this explanation isn't clear, neither was the film.) Joan played the man's counterpart girlfriend who is dying of heart disease. It was a spoof and was seen as 'great fun' by the *London Sunday Telegraph*. *Variety* was only one of the papers that loved Joan's performance: 'Joan Collins has rarely been better.... Beautifully gowned throughout and looking gorgeous, she acts with warmth.'

This was followed by *Terror from Under the House* and *Fear in the Night*, for which the London *Evening Standard* said 'Miss Collins [is] always better than her material.' *Tales from the Crypt*, based on the horror-comic books of the fifties, was next, and consisted of five separate stories. The film had an all-star cast including Ralph Richardson and Peter Cushing, and the critics loved it. 'Everything works nastily to awe and disgust us,' *The Village Voice* said, and the New York *Daily News* added that it was 'gruesome, hair-raising fun that guarantees insomnia'. The first episode was the one in which Joan starred, and it was generally seen as the best. Joan played a woman who killed her husband, made it look like an accident, and was eventually strangled to death by a homicidal maniac dressed as Santa Claus. 'Joan Collins [is] transformed into a cold-as-ice damned murderess,' one of the reviews said.

In short, Joan was acting better than she had ever acted in her life. If one is to take her word for it, one would have to go along with her theory that one cannot mature as an actress until one matures as a person. She was happier than she had ever been in her life and had a perfect fix on what she was doing. 'None of these films was by any means either a box-office bonanza or a work of art, but an actor acts and I needed the bread,' she said a few years ago, very realistically. 'I was a survivor,' she added. 'And thanks to Ron I had faith in myself as last.'

She and Ron married in March 1972. In June Joan gave birth to Katyana Kennedy Kass, 'Katy'. The extended Kass family bought a house in London and actually lived in it – for the first time since she'd left her parents' house Joan was living in her own home! Everything was working out. Around this time Joan's father remarried (a woman, coincidentally, about Joan's age) and had another child. Joan's feelings for and about him were finally being resolved, and her own happiness left plenty of room for her to understand him better.

In 1972 Joan was signed to star in an American television adaptation of *The Man Who Came to Dinner*, to be filmed in England. The Hallmark Hall of Fame was as prestigious a television show as existed at the time, and Joan was to play Lorraine Sheldon, a 'super-sexpot actress', with some great comic lines and a real flair for the flashy. The title role was to be played by Orson Welles, who had begun his film career as a legend and had remained one. His performance was so bad (Joan reports that he read every one of his lines from a cue card and terrorized the other actors), or so most of the critics felt, that the show wasn't particularly successful. The reviews for Joan, however, were excellent. She was finally doing comedy, and she had been right – she had a definite flair for it.

Then two bad movies followed: *Tales That Witness Madness* and *Dark Places*. In the first, Joan was in an eighteen-minute episode in which she played the wife of a man who brings a tree into their home and falls in love with it. She tells her husband that either the tree goes or she goes. She went. One of the other episodes starred Kim Novak, making a sort of 'comeback' to the screen. *The Village Voice* said about the film: 'The humor lacks wit, the horror lacks poetry. Kim Novak's reappearance is easily eclipsed by Joan Collins, who still looks a knockout two decades after *Land of the Pharaohs*.' The interesting thing here is not that Joan was being appreciated, but that all of her American films had been so unimportant, and so unmemorable (as she had always known), that the reviewer's first thoughts had been of Joan's first American film! It was, sadly, as if the twenty-five or so films in between hadn't mattered. And in fact, they hadn't.

Dark Places was an even worse film. It was a psychic-possession thriller that *Variety* called 'of no distinction, bound for TV'. This, from *Variety* in 1974, was the greatest curse imaginable. *The Bawdy Adventures of Tom Jones*, called by the *Los Angeles Times* a 'cheap, crude, sexed-up rehash' of the 1962 Tony Richardson classic with Albert Finney, was a quick way for Joan to earn some money and for the film to have a 'star' name. The role of Black Bess, a highwaywoman, was tiny, and it was created for Joan. Once again the critics liked the way she looked, but cared little (or nothing) for the movie.

Ron, too, realized that Joan's talent lay with comedy. In addition to being president of Warner Bros. Records in the United Kingdom, he was producing films. He had secured the rights to Noël Coward's *Fallen Angels*, which had been seen in New York in 1927 with Tallulah Bankhead and Edna Best. Joan starred along with Susannah York (Joan acted as casting director), and the show was made for British television. It was shown over Christmas 1974, and the reviews were stunning.

The Rank Organization called her back to do another horror movie called *The Devil Within Her*, and always the trouper, she agreed. She played a nightclub stripper (not bad for a woman of forty-one) who is cursed by a dwarf she rejects, to bear a devil child who goes on a killing spree. *The New York Times* called it 'a smear to dwarfs', and most of the other reviews were equally appalling. Once again, however, in her new maturity, Joan came out 'looking and acting splendidly', as *Variety* put it.

With everything coming up roses, it was left to nothing less formidable than the British government to destroy the happiness the Kasses and, finally, Joan, had found. In 1975 the tax situation became so bad that many wealthy people in the creative arts (and other fields), including Joan and her family, had to leave England or get soaked to the bone. The Kasses uprooted and once more Joan returned to Hollywood.

9
The Collins Girls – Together Again for the First Time

In essence, it was Ron who talked Joan into having the family move back to the United States. 'I fought it tooth and nail,' Joan has since said. She fought, but she lost. She had finally achieved everything she had wanted in London – she loved her husband and children, and she was being acknowledged for the rather good actress she had always claimed to be. She hated being back in Hollywood despite the flash and dash of their lives. They had bought a magnificent home in Trousdale with marble floors and a tennis court, but it had been fourteen years since Joan had been a regular on the Hollywood scene. She experienced, for the first time, ageism – many people were considering the forty-two-year-old star to be over-the-hill. Still, she managed to land guest shots on several television shows, among them *Baretta*, *Mission: Impossible*, *Policewoman*, and *Batman*. She earned about $2,500 an episode, a relatively paltry sum when it is seen beside the $80,000 a year she had been earning in 1959.

Ron was lured away from his position as president of Warner Bros. Records in Britain by whiskey-heir Edgar Bronfman to head his new film company, Sagittarius. That went well for a while. The Kasses socialized with Edgar and his current lady friend, and Edgar became Katy's godfather. Then one day, without warning, Edgar fired Ron and closed the company down. The Kasses sold their home and moved. Their finances needed bolstering and Joan was forced to take on movie assignments she hated, such as the filmed-in-Spain *The Great Adventure* with Jack Palance, which was a mess. However, it earned her ten or fifteen thousand dollars, which they desperately needed. Joan's desire to stay in London despite the tax situation had been well-founded; with the new pressures on the family her marriage began to fall apart.

In 1976 Joan began to look elsewhere for her happiness. She went to a series of 'human potential exploration' sessions (remember, this *is* California) with a group called 'Actualizations', headed by an Australian named Stewart Emory. She stood up before the assembled throng and announced that her marriage was a 'fiasco'. She told them how Ron had changed since he hadn't been working and how unhappy she was. Money was a real problem – the $1,250 a month Tony Newley was paying her for child support wasn't enough considering the fact that neither she nor Ron was working regularly. Emory told her to 'stand by her man', to quote a country-and-western standard. Nothing was giving Joan any satisfaction or happiness.

The television show that pushed her over the edge, that forced her to take matters into her own hands, was *Starsky and Hutch*, which she filmed on location in Hawaii in the summer of 1976. She had just finished making a miniseries for NBC called *The Moneychangers*. To get the role she had had to chop ten years off her age, and she regarded her pay as being less than generous. She thought she had hit rock bottom, but she was treated so badly on location in Hawaii that it paled by comparison. She didn't have her own dressing room, she was overexposed to the sun, she was badly costumed. The crew and producers couldn't have cared less. 'I felt that this was not how I was going to end my career – doing TV, being herded around and hearing "Joan *who*?" she told a *Rolling Stone* interviewer recently. 'It was then that I thought of *The Stud*.'

The Stud was her sister Jackie's best-selling novel that had been published in 1970. Jackie had undergone vast changes in the intervening years. In 1960, when she was still trying to become an actress, a 'star', she had changed her name to Lynn Curtis, and then Jackie Douglas. She told the press that she was 'sick and tired of being called Joan Collins's sister'. She had continued to appear in terrible movies, had married a British fashion executive, and had had a daughter. Her husband, however, was addicted to drugs, and the marriage did not last. (He died in 1968 of a drug overdose.) She had always flirted with the idea of writing (as a child, she had written stories Joan had illustrated), and when she married Oscar Lerman in 1966 he was impressed enough with her work to convince her that she should give up acting and concentrate on her writing. It was a fortuitous decision. Her first novel, *The World Is Full of Married Men*, was sexy and frank, a great success, and was banned in Australia. 'What's the matter,' Jackie asked, 'don't you have married men [there?]' The book was designed to 'get a dig at men', and it worked. Her writing career took off as fast as her acting career had not taken off, and she stopped living in Joan's shadow. Critic Tom Driberg, in *The Guardian*, said he 'had never read a nastier novel'. Jackie, it seems, was getting revenge on all the men she knew and all the hypocrisy they ever perpetrated. By the time she wrote *The Stud*, she was a household name in England and was beginning to be one in America.

When *The Stud* came out, it was considered 'mildly pornographic' (Jackie, however, claims that all of her novels are very moralistic) and apparently it was just what Joan had been looking for. In September of 1976 Joan was collecting unemployment insurance, had gotten into taking care of herself with an exercise guru in West Hollywood, and was trying to peddle *The Stud* to backers. 'Tom Jones has agreed to play the stud,' she told *Women's Wear Daily*. 'I will play an extremely elegant rich nymphomaniac who puts him in business. I started at the age of sixteen playing bad girls. Later I got to play some nice ones. But my sister says "you're only good when you play bitches."' Whether this was Jackie the sibling or Jackie the casting director speaking we'll never know. As it turns out, she seems to have been right.

In between traveling from coast to coast trying to sell *The Stud*, Joan got a much needed (for the money, at least) part in *Empire of the Ants*. It was called 'definitely the worst ant movie ever made' by one critic, and Joan agrees that filming in the Florida swamps in November and December was one of the most disgusting jobs she has ever had. *The New York Times* found the 'special effects were artificial and unexciting', and the *Soho News* said it was 'trash without being serious about it'. For the most part Joan escaped critically unscathed, with just a bit of praise: *Variety* said: 'Collins gets right down there in the swamp mud with all the others, a good trouper heading a cast that at least rates a nod for physical endurance.' Faint praise, but at least she (unlike the character she played) got out alive.

She continued to try to peddle *The Stud*, convinced that 'it would reactivate [her] career [and] be a commercial success.'

Early in 1977 Joan was asked to play a blackmailer in director Michael Winner's remake of the 1946 classic *The Big Sleep*. Once again needing the money and ever more unhappy and frustrated with Ron, she agreed. Lew Grade, Joan's godfather, was the producer – they were working together at last. The reviewers almost unanimously hated Winner's directing and claimed that the actors got lost in the shuffle. Joan's reviews ranged from 'does a nice bit' to 'hangs around to decorate the scenery', with 'still looks smashing' somewhere in between.

Never the prima donna when it came to keeping bread on the table – and often at her best when faced with a crisis – Joan kept working. She spent a good deal of the early part of 1977 in Europe, trying to sell *The Stud*, making a film in Italy called *Poliziotto Senza Paura* and finally winding up at the Cannes Film Festival in May. She was sorry to be away from her children but was just as pleased to be removed from Ron, who had gained an enormous amount of weight, and who she suspected was taking some kind of drugs. She had learned from Jackie's terrible experience to be wary of drugs and wouldn't go near them herself, but there was nothing she could do for Ron. She spent her time, therefore, trying to make money. Literary agent Irving (Swifty) Lazar contacted her and suggested she write her memoirs. She needed the money, had had a pretty exciting and lusty life, and agreed. Tentatively calling it *I Was a Stranger*, Joan began work on it.

At Cannes, she finally struck gold. She was there ostensibly to promote *Empire of the Ants* (a practically impossible assignment) and pitched *The Stud* to everyone she met. Finally she met George Walker, head of Brent-Walker Productions, and presented him with the script Jackie had written. Ron and Oscar Lerman, Jackie's husband, coproduced, and filming began in June. Joan's salary was $25,000; the film eventually earned $30,000,000! 'The Collins Sisters', as they began to be called (Jackie hated that one too), had made it – together.

10

Sex and Eroticism

Joan's decisions to appear in *The Stud* and to write her memoirs (the title of which was changed to *Past Imperfect*) turned out to be two of the most important she has ever made, at least with regard to her career. They both made her rich, and they both made her famous – or infamous, if one wants to look at it that way. It might be said that once Joan took control of her life, she *really* took control of her life, and wound up strongly and steadily on the road to the real stardom that had managed to elude her for the previous twenty-five years.

The Stud and *Past Imperfect* both hit Britain at almost the same time. The effect they had on the public was practically that of a volcanic eruption, but in somewhat different ways. Joan had always been called 'Britain's Bad Girl', 'The Coffee Bar Jezebel', and other snappy names, but this time, at last, she was doing it to herself. With regard to *The Stud*, she has said, 'I wanted to make it successful; that's why I exploited myself. I thought it would get me back on the track of being a commercial actress. I deliberately exploited myself. Totally.' The famous (or, once again, infamous) 'sex-on-a-swing' shot and Joan's nudity clinched it. Her only concern over the reactions of others, she told *Playboy* later, was 'what [her] father would think'. In fact, he found her 'attractive', she reported.

'The character I played did to men what men have been doing to women for thousands of years.' She and Jackie were trying to turn what *The New York Times* called 'illiterate ... antierotic [and] amateurish' and *Variety* labeled 'banal' into a social statement. They didn't succeed, of course, but the side effects were far more important.

Joan told the New York *Daily News* in September of 1979 that her 'career wasn't going anywhere after having done fifty motion pictures and twenty-five TV shows. This film made me a household word again in England and has brought me once again to the attention of producers.' She was right. Offers came pouring in. Time changes people, and the fact that Joan had told Earl Wilson in 1957 that she would never do commercials because she would 'feel like a complete hypocrite' did not stop her from accepting a very lucrative contract from Cinzano to appear in their British television and print ads. Nor did it stop her from promoting her new line of women's jeans. And as long as she was hot, she decided to meet her contract obligations with Brent-Walker to do a sequel to *The Stud* called *The Bitch.*

Before that, however, she returned to the United States to make *Zero to Sixty*, which was directed by and co-starred Darren McGavin. It was hardly even reviewed and was taken out of distribution very quickly. Far more important for her in the early part of 1978 was the publication of *Past Imperfect.*

Joan got an incredible amount of flak over what Liz Smith called her 'kiss everybody and tell everything' autobiography. 'I got insulted on television shows.... It was as if I had done something obscene. And all I was doing was being honest,' Joan told *Playboy* magazine recently. Warner Books in the United States had paid Joan a handsome $100,000 to publish the book in America, and she returned the advance. 'It was a mistake,' she told *People* magazine in December of 1982. 'My countrymen sneered so much I gave back [the advance] to not have it come out in the United States. I must say writing it seemed like a good idea at the time.' What really seems to have motivated Joan to write it was money (as she had said). What she wasn't doing when she wrote it was thinking of the consequences it would have on her family life.

Joan decided not to permit the publication of *Past Imperfect* in the United States for a variety of reasons. Liz Smith reported that 'husband Ron Kass said he'd take their daughter and leave if she did'. This may or may not be true, because at the time of the book's publication in America, the couple had split up anyway. The decision couldn't have been based on Joan's desire to be less 'notorious'; that was always her calling card and was working particularly well at this point. 'The only person who was unhappy was my ex-husband [Newley],' she told the *Daily News* in September of 1979. 'Since we weren't talking before it came out, there'd be no reason we'd be talking afterwards.' This, too, appears to be only half true.

If one had to make an educated guess as to why Joan refused to have that unexpurgated version of *Past Imperfect* published again, in the United States, one would guess that Tara and Sacha had something to do with the decision. In the American version of the book, published several years after the British, Joan writes: 'We [she and Ron] decided that Tara and Sacha should stay with [Newley] and his new wife while I was working in England. The children decided that life at the Newleys' was more settled than life at the Kasses' and opted for living permanently with Tony.' This, plain and simple, is a whitewash of the situation. For a woman known for her honesty, it is odd that she left out the following information, reported in the *New York Post*, as a news article (rather than as a bit of gossip):

> April 25, 1978. It isn't easy being a mother. That's the lesson learned by poor Joan Collins whose two children by

Anthony Newley recently announced they'd had it with Mummy and want to go live with Daddy. And what had Mummy done? Nothing worse than write her embarrassingly intimate memoirs, which told the world, in the most detailed terms, all about her numerous liaisons with famous gents. Joanie, you see, doesn't feel she has to apologize for anything she's done in her life (or in her book). But her children: Sacha, 11, and Tara, 13, who are old enough to understand (and have friends who understand) such things, responded by moving in with Newley, who also lives in Beverly Hills. The upshot is that Joan and Tony have had to work out a joint custody arrangement.

'... I resent people peering at me all the time, chronicling my dates, making my personal life public property,' Joan had told an interviewer back in 1962 in the *New York Post.* In order to stop other people from cashing in on her, therefore, she had cashed in on herself by writing her memoirs. Her 'self-exploitation' was at its peak when she wrote *Past Imperfect.*

One must assume that Joan was thinking only of her flagging career at the time she agreed to publish her memoirs and that she assumed, wrongly, that they would have little or no effect on her children. It is obvious that she has acknowledged her mistake, for the version of *Past Imperfect* that was eventually published in the United States was far tamer, less graphic in its discussions of her sexuality, and most important, was infinitely more gentle to Newley. One would think that this has everything to do with her children, but in addition, the fact is that in the six years between the publication of the first and second versions of the book Joan had become a superstar and wanted to present a somewhat more genteel version of herself to the public.

After making *Game for Vultures* in South Africa and an episode for Anglia TV's *Roald Dahl's Tales of the Unexpected*, Joan began work on *The Bitch*. It turned out to be a putrid imitation of *The Stud*, even more distasteful and tacky, poorly made, and badly thought out. She was being packaged solely for money, but since she had agreed to do the film, she did. Sadly, it turned her into somewhat of a joke in England. The ad campaign concentrated on 'tits and ass', and the printed ads read 'Joan Collins *is* the Bitch.' She hated it, but luckily it didn't irrevocably harm her career.

She was signed to make *Sunburn*, a star vehicle designed for Farrah Fawcett-Majors, fresh from her success as one of Charlie's angels and the most popular poster girl in America. Almost all of the reviews focused on Farrah, but Joan – as always – proved to be impossible to ignore. The *Daily News* praised her 'comic zest'; *The Village Voice* said she 'slithers cheerfully'; and the *Soho News*, which liked the movie, said that Joan 'was another reason' to see it. On the negative side, *The New York Times* said 'Miss Collins's aggressive nymphomaniac routine is supposed to be funny this time. It's not.' None of this matters if one considers one of the really ironic lines in the movie. The character played by Farrah, attempting to be critical or bitchy toward Joan, says about her: 'She must be at least forty.' Joan was forty-seven at the time.

Happily, Joan returned to work in the theatre for the summer of 1980. Despite the fact (or perhaps because of the fact) that she was practically considered a scarlet woman in Britain, the Chichester Festival Arts Theatre invited her to perform in *The Last of Mrs Cheyney*, a comedy by Frederick Lonsdale. Joan played a would-be jewel thief, and the reviews were good. *Variety* said she gave 'an acceptable performance that won't disappoint her fans'. It became the highest-grossing show in the Festival's nineteen-year history, selling out even at notoriously badly attended matinees. Ron took over the promotion of Joan and the show. He beefed up her radio, TV,

Joan made a stage appearance in London's West End some months after her daughter Katy's near-fatal accident. Joan is still lovely, despite the obvious toll taken by the ordeal of nursing her injured daughter back to health.

Three years later (1983) Joan arrived at London's Heathrow Airport with injured husband Kass and now-well daughter Katy, busily denying rumours of a rift in their marriage. Only months later they were separated. (*Photos on these pages credited to AP/Wide World Photos*)

After years of being good in lousy roles Joan finally landed the part she was destined to play – Alexis in *Dynasty*.

Joan poses with Dynasty costars Linda Evans and John Forsythe at an unveiling of 'Collins', a limited edition serigraph by artist Patrick Nagel.

Among other momentous events of 1983 Joan Collins got her own star in the Hollywood Walk of Fame.

Despite the demands of a career Joan today remains close to her children.

She is seen here with Tara . . .

. . . and with Sacha . . .

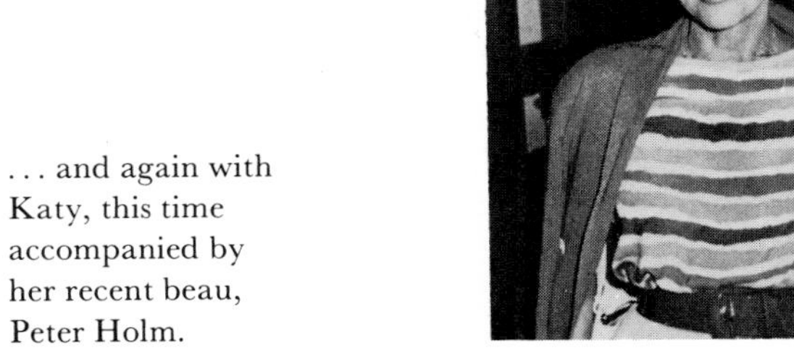

(*Photos on these pages credited to AP/Wide World Photos*)

. . . and again with Katy, this time accompanied by her recent beau, Peter Holm.

And in 1984 America made Joan Collins a best-selling author. (*AP/Wide World Photos*)

Despite some strange publicity shots Joan Collins was unmistakably beautiful. (*Museum of Modern Art/Film Stills Archive*)

For those who were keeping score, there was a period when Joan was involved with Warren Beatty (seen here being introduced to England's Princess Margaret). When marriage did not happen, they split, he taking up with actress Natalie Wood, and she, so the gossip columnists alleged, with . . .

. . . Robert Wagner, estranged husband of Wood. Here he and Joan are seen together on a date in England, where both were making films. (*AP/Wide World Photos*)

It was, however, British musical star Anthony Newley who finally captured Joan's heart and became her second husband. They posed for photographers at New York's El Morocco on the day of their wedding.

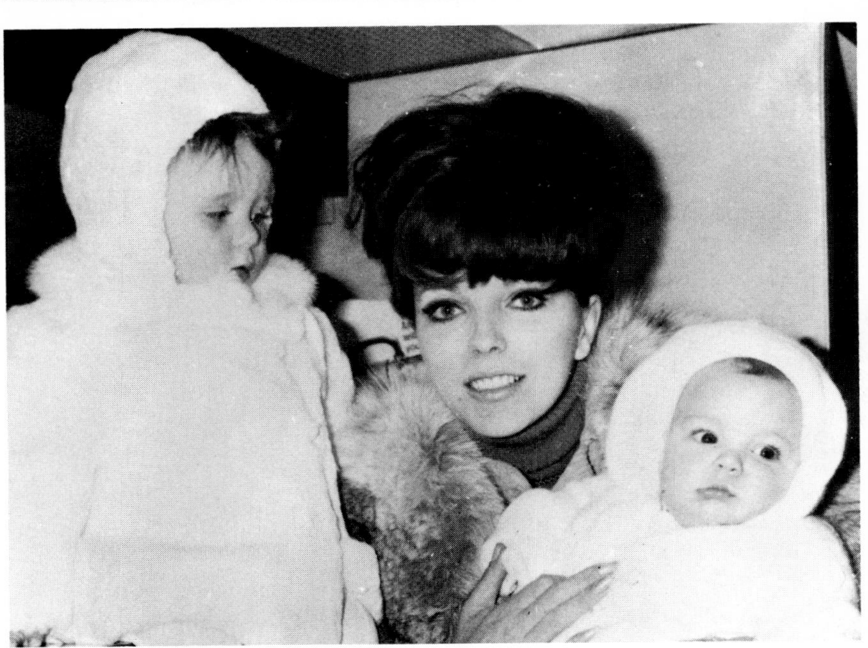

Joan had two children by Anthony Newley – Tara (here age two) and Sacha (four months). Despite her love for her children, Joan was unable to keep the marriage together. (*AP/Wide World Photos*)

In 1971 Joan married businessman Ron Kass. Here she is seen with their daughter, Katy, on location in Italy for an entirely forgettable film, *The Referee.*

While her marriage to Kass had its ups and downs, Joan's career consisted of one long low point. Here she manages to remain beautiful while appearing as a murderous wife in the British horror film *Tales from the Crypt.*

It was a film based on her sister Jackie's best-selling and steamy novel *The Stud* that finally brought Joan back into the celluloid limelight. This publicity photo went out with a caption heralding the beginning of a search for 'five male supermen' to costar with Joan in a sequel to *The Stud*, aptly titled *The Bitch.*

and press appearances, and changed the repellent *Bitch* posters to conform more with Joan's image in the play. Triumph Productions, thrilled by the summer run of the play, decided to mount it in London's West End. Joan had written a beauty book that was scheduled for release in October, with a spoken-word version to be issued by Warwick Records at the same time. As a 'close pal' reported in *Cosmopolitan*. '[Ron] constantly promoted her as if he were her personal manager.... [He] never wavered in his belief in her. He really got her back on the ball again.' Despite their unhappy home lives, the Kasses were becoming enormously successful. Ron was her true mentor. The only thing they weren't together was happy.

Sacha and Tara had come back to live with the Kasses for the summer, and by this time Joan had announced her plans to stop the publication of her book in America. She and Tara and Ron had to go to Paris to meet with the legendary Erté, who had agreed to do the costumes for the West End production of *The Last of Mrs Cheyney*. They left on August 1. The following day, a parent's nightmare came true.

11
Katy

If one is superstitious, one knows that when things are going well, they will change, usually *not* for the better. Granted, Joan's marriage to Ron Kass was anything but a storybook romance by the summer of 1980. They still looked great together; he was working (albeit through and with her), but much of the love on which their relationship had been based was gone. She still suspected that he was taking drugs, they argued too often to assure happiness, and he was unhappy about the publication of her book. On the other hand, Joan was working in theatre and she had been able (at least partially) to lose the 'scarlet woman' stigma that accompanied her appearances in *The Stud* and *The Bitch*. She was making good money from the Cinzano commercials. The home videos of *The Stud* and *The Bitch* were, according to *Variety*, the two top-selling cassettes in the United States in August of that year. She was about to be costumed by a man who designed the most elegant fashions in the world, to perform in a hit play on one of the world's most prestigious stretches of theatrical activity in the world. Something dreadful, if one is superstitious, had to happen. And it did.

'You cannot envision what it's like to see your child in a coma in an intensive care ward, with her head shaved and tubes coming out of everywhere, eyes closed, not moving at all . . .' Joan was finally able to tell *People* magazine in November of 1981, more than a year after her daughter Katy was almost killed when she was struck by a car. Indeed, most of us cannot envision what it's like, and hopefully will never have to.

The Kasses received a phone call in Paris at 2 A.M. on August 2, a matter of hours after they had left England. Katy, who had been staying with a friend in the Berkshire countryside, had been hit by a car and had suffered a critical head injury. Joan and Ron had to get back to England as quickly as they could. There were no flights. Joan called everyone she knew, including her father. He came to her rescue with the name Roger Whittaker, a family friend with a private plane. Whittaker agreed to meet them at Le Bourget Airport at 5.30 A.M. The three and a half hours seemed like months; guilt, anxiety, fear, all mixed together. Joan screamed with fear and grief. They arrived at Le Bourget and flew to London Airport, arriving at dawn. The doctors told Ron and Joan that Katy's chances of survival were sixty to forty – against. They borrowed a mobile home from friends and camped out in the hospital's parking lot. 'Katy's not going to die. She's absolutely not!' Joan and Ron swore.

Katy was in a coma for forty-two days. After the eighth day she opened her eyes, but they were blank. By the end of the second week she had lost twenty pounds. She was so weak and pale that people who saw her were driven to tears. At one point an intern at the hospital told Joan not to bother herself about Katy – she wasn't going to get any better. Joan took him outside and blew up at him, then went back to the parked van and punched the wall so hard, with such hysterical force, that her wrist had to be bandaged.

Joan and Ron never stopped talking to Katy, never stopped stimulating her. Joan felt that 'every day you're in a coma you're losing some more of life'; nonetheless, her natural optimism kept her working for Katy. For six weeks she and Ron never stopped talking to Katy, never stopped playing music for her, never stopped touching her, never stopped giving her things to smell, things like lemons, perfume, onions. They provided her every stimulus they could. They would not let her die. They watched her in physiotherapy; she was like 'a little animal', a rag doll.

On September 13, Katy came home, but still had no reactions, no real life. On the 18th, Ron and Joan were sharing a joke and Joan used the word *shit*. Katy laughed, and Ron and Joan knew that she understood, even if she couldn't communicate. They were enormously relieved, but still terrified. Ron had been keeping the truth from Joan, truth the doctors had told him but couldn't tell her. That truth was that Katy could have brain damage and might have to be institutionalized. Without that knowledge Joan went on as she felt, with Ron, that with God's help, Katy would get better.

A week after they realized she could understand what was being said, she spoke her first word in two months – *horseshoe*. A few weeks later she took her first 'new' steps, and a bit later she wrote her first 'new' words: 'Dear Mommy and Daddy, I love you very much.' This note was handed to Joan on opening night, backstage, at the West End production of *The Last of Mrs Cheyney*. It was the greatest bouquet an actress had ever received, and the greatest gift a mother could want.

Joan and Ron's marriage was still deteriorating, but Katy's accident, and their mutual grief, love, and responsibility, forced them to put their own problems on hold while Katy recovered. As it turned out, *The Last of Mrs Cheyney* was not the success everyone had hoped it would be, and to make matters worse, Joan and Ron had put some of their own money into the production as an investment. In addition, Joan had foolishly signed a contract that had a clause in it stating that in the event that the show should begin to lose money, her salary had to go towards making up the difference!

The play closed in January and Joan went to Los Angeles to sell their home, which they hadn't lived in for over a year. Ron had become weaker and weaker about his responsibilities and Joan discovered that they were in debt far more than he had led her to believe. They had by now been married for almost ten years and the prospect of a third failed marriage was almost more than she could abide. She vacillated between wanting a divorce and hoping the marriage could be saved. If only Ron were to get work, pay attention to details, etc. If only. . . .

Joan the worker, the survivor, was offered a guest spot on Aaron Spelling's *Fantasy Island* for TV, and despite her promise to herself after the catastrophic *Starsky and Hutch* episode, she needed the money and accepted it. Besides that, she was to play Cleopatra in the episode – at last! The experience was a pleasant one, but Joan still felt that the stage was her medium.

Back in London, in their Georgian house with many rooms and a garden in which Katy could play, Joan and Ron tried to keep their marriage intact. Joan played in a thriller called *Murder in Mind* in Guildford, and performed with her arm in a cast, the result of a fall down a flight of stairs a few nights earlier. The trouper, and, sadly, the bread-winner, had to keep working. The play was a moderate success, and when it closed, Triumph Productions planned a ten-week tour of the play, with Joan, all around England.

In July the family went to Marbella, Spain, for a vacation. Katy was recovering nicely, but still needed constant care, a speech therapist, and a great deal of time before she would be considered 'well'. Joan received a phone call from her agent, Tom Korman, offering her some work in Hollywood. It was the last thing she wanted, to move again, and the work was for a night-time soap opera that had started out as fifty-fourth in the ratings. Sophia Loren, Elizabeth Taylor, and Raquel Welch had been considered for the part. Korman insisted that the part was a juicy one and could make Joan a star again. Tempted, Joan agreed to think about it. The show was called *Dynasty*.

12

Princess Nellifer Goes to Denver

Richard and Esther Shapiro met in a UCLA writing class in 1956 and were married four years later. They wrote, together and separately, but unsuccessfully, for a few years, and then in the sixties they wrote for shows like *Bonanza* and *Route 66*. Richard also wrote several episodes of the Raymond Burr crime show *Ironsides*.

In 1969 they were offered a job writing for a daytime soap opera called *Love of Life*, for $3,000 a week. While enjoying their newfound wealth, they found the pressures of turning out scripts day after day too grueling and soon resigned their assignment. They continued to write for television, but like most writers, they had little or no control over the finished product, since that was the bailiwick of producers. After a stint in Europe they returned to the United States and Esther became an ABC vice-president for miniseries and produced serious works – *Masada* and *Inside the Third Reich*, to name two. In 1979 executive producer Aaron Spelling, who had become rich and famous with *The Love Boat*, *Charlie's Angels*, and several other immensely popular prime-time television shows, was looking for an answer to the success CBS was having with *Dallas*, and he thought of the Shapiros. They agreed to work for him, but only if they could produce as well as write.

'We wanted an oil-based family and chose Denver because

we like writing about middle America,' Esther explains. 'I like to create characters who are always trying to gain control of their lives.' The way it has worked out, Richard, who has a better ear for the spoken word, does most of the writing, and Esther acts as the businesswoman and casting director. They decided to call the show *Dynasty*, and cast veteran actor John Forsythe in the pivotal role of Blake Carrington, oil billionaire, and Linda Evans, certainly one of the world's most beautiful women and a veteran of many successful television shows, as his then-wife-to-be, Krystle. Carrington was to be mysteriously divorced, with his two children living, more or less, with him, rather than with their mother, whoever she might be. Steven, his son, was to be a pretty-poorly-closeted homosexual, and Fallon, his daughter, a playgirl who has just returned from a trip around the world, during which she seduced as many men as possible. Their life-style was to be epic: a mansion with rooms too numerous to count (close to fifty are hinted at); Rolls-Royces in the multicar garage; a stable of horses; dozens of servants, maids, and cooks; and a majordomo overseeing the help. Champagne was to flow like water, caviar to be as much in evidence as sand on a beach. In short, the stuff dreams are made of.

The basic problem with the first season of *Dynasty*, which left it eventually at a rather paltry thirty-eighth in the ratings (especially paltry for Aaron Spelling, who was accustomed to ratings in the single digits), was that there were no adversaries, no villains. The enormous success of *Dallas* was due, in large part, to the presence of Larry Hagman as J.R. Ewing, the richest villain to come down the pike in years. He had become the man America (and Europe, in syndication) loved to hate.

In *Dynasty*'s first season there was plenty of action, but not nearly enough tension – and no real hatred. Krystle and Blake got married; Fallon, who initially hated and resented Krystle, learned to love and respect her (as haven't we all). She then married the enormously wealthy and charming Jeff Colby, nephew of Blake's business associate and fellow-extremely-rich-person Cecil Colby. Steven, if no one else, came to terms with his homosexuality after a brief affair with the vaguely disturbed Claudia Blaisdel. Another problem the show had besides lack of tension was that Blake wasn't perfect – he occasionally did villainous things and was predisposed to drink. He had his chauffeur beaten up in one episode and was seen ripping Krystle's clothes off in another. But he was supposed to be the hero, a man with flaws, but nevertheless a good man. When he accidentally killed his son Steven's lover, Ted Dinard, and had to go on trial, there was plenty of tension created, but it left the viewers confused, not sure if they were meant to side with him. If their hero was going to jail, what kind of a hero was he? What did they have to judge him against? Watching a basically good man with rather significant flaws is not the stuff of which great soap opera is made.

In the first season's final episode Claudia Blaisdel and her daughter had a car accident and her husband, Matthew, was thrown in jail, but viewers couldn't have cared less about them. Blake testified under oath that Ted Dinard's death was an accident and that he loved his son Steven despite his past life, his 'life-style', as it is always referred to on the show. Then the prosecution called a surprise witness. She was Blake's first wife, who had not been heard from since she deserted the children many years before. She was sworn in to testify against Blake, leaving the viewers watching, but not glued, and the ratings at thirty-eight. Both she and her testimony had to be nothing short of spectacular. As it turns out, they were.

Spelling and the Shapiros began their search for the perfect actress to play the mysterious woman. The character was originally to be called Madeline, but the name was later changed to the more exotic-sounding Alexis. For the season's final episode, the cliff-hanger, the Shapiros had put an actress into a white suit, a hat, and a veil, and photographed her in such a way as to make certain that her face wasn't seen. While Sophia Loren and Raquel Welch were being considered, Esther Shapiro was holding out for Joan Collins. However, she had to convince the other people involved with the show that Joan was right for the part.

'Joan was older,' Shapiro explained recently, 'and the reaction was strong against her. People felt her accent would not be understood and they thought she was over the hill. But I thought she was the only person for the role. She has humor, and I felt the part could not work without humor. And Alexis had to be – and Joan is – a great beauty.'

'I'm certain that it didn't hurt my chances for this part for the producers to know that I was the biggest movie star in England,' Joan said recently, with a dazzling lack of modesty. 'That had to make an impression.' Indeed it did, but it wasn't as easy for Joan to take the part as one might assume. She *had* promised herself to Triumph Productions for a ten-week run of the play *Murder in Mind*, and they were out to make her true to her word. They pleaded, cajoled, and finally threatened, but Joan stood firm. She knew that this TV role was the greatest chance she had ever been offered and that she would be a fool to turn it down. The role was wonderful even if the series was a flop (or a near-flop), and television was a perfect way of rejuvenating her American career. (She had taken to riding around in Los Angeles with a license plate that read 'Joan who?' a couple of years before. Perhaps now it wouldn't be necessary.) Even if the series only lasted for six months, she figured that the exposure and the money would be great. Furthermore, with Sacha and Tara at school, Katy was the Kasses' only concern, and the California sunshine was recommended more highly than the London mist for recovery. Triumph Productions be damned; the Kasses went to California in August for Joan to begin work on *Dynasty*, as Alexis Morrell Carrington.

It was pretty clear from the opening episode that Joan had landed in a gold mine, and that she was going to make the best of a great part. The character Alexis was even more predatory than Princess Nellifer had been as she had 'clawed her way to the throne' in *The Land of the Pharaohs*. A predatory girl can never be taken as seriously as a predatory woman, and Joan, at the age of forty-eight, was all woman, and a woman in her prime at that. 'Collins,' critic James Wolcott wrote in *New York* magazine halfway through Joan's first season on the show, 'is the sort of woman who seems born to swing from chandeliers as geysers of freshly popped champagne flare in tribute.' The actress who had so loathed being labeled 'the bitch' had found herself a role that was beyond that epithet – 'super-bitch' and 'bitch-goddess' seem more appropriate.

In that first season Alexis Carrington performed a series of dastardly deeds that would become legendary in the annals of television villainy.

At Blake's trial Alexis tells the jury that Blake has payed her $250,000 a year for the past several years not to see her children. This could have been seen as sympathetic, but that wasn't what the Shapiros had in mind, and that wasn't the way Joan played it. Her testimony causes angelic Krystle to leave the courtroom in horror, and anyone who can do that is on the dark side of good. Joan/Alexis's slithery style also foreboded evil, and the impression was right. J.R. Ewing was going to have a run for his money. When, in the season's second episode, Alexis tells Blake 'This studio is mine ... I'm moving in,' it's apparent that she means not only moving into the Carrington property, but moving into the Twentieth Century-Fox Studios where *Dynasty* is taped as well. In a subsequent episode she is cruel to her daughter, Fallon, for continuing to love Blake. Then she plays on Steven's weaknesses and tells him that Fallon is not Blake's legitimate daughter (Steven cannot believe this and Alexis says, 'Believe it or not darling, it's true,' and walks out). It, of course, turns out to be a lie. Then she tells Cecil Colby that Fallon is *his* daughter; she plays on Blake's sympathies and tries to seduce him (if for no other reason than to upset Krystle); hires a private investigator to pry into Krystle's past; tries (successfully) to turn Steven against Blake; and in mid-season, shoots a gun into the air to scare the horse Krystle is riding, so that the horse throws Krystle, causing her to lose the baby she's carrying. What kind of a woman would do that? Lady Macbeth? Princess Nellifer grown up? Precisely.

The role Joan was playing became more notorious than Joan had ever been; indeed it is the only role in her career that has overshadowed her private life. In November of 1981 Joan was invited to appear in 'The Night of 100 Stars' at Radio City Music Hall in New York. It was clear that after almost twenty-nine years in show business, Joan had arrived. If there had ever been any doubts about whether or not Joan Collins was a 'star', they disappeared that night.

Her private life, however, was not going quite so well. Her marriage was still on the rocks. She and Ron were not getting along at all, but had agreed to remain together and try to work things out as long as Katy was ill. Katy was improving daily, but the marriage wasn't. Katy begged them to stop fighting.

The plot thickened on *Dynasty* as well. Alexis causes her daughter, Fallon, such grief that she smashes her car into a wall and her baby is born prematurely. She finds out that Krystle has been married before, that the divorce wasn't altogether legal, and demands to have the husband brought to her. She decides to marry Cecil Colby, Blake's business rival, as a first step toward destroying Blake. In an episode still considered extraordinarily racy for prime-time television, Alexis and Cecil are making love and he suffers a heart attack. It is before their wedding and if he dies, she cannot get her hands (should we say 'claws?') on his money. In a piece of vicious dialogue that pushed *Dynasty* into the top-ten-rated television shows in the nation, a monstrous Alexis screams, 'Don't you dare die on me, Cecil! You can't die on me. I need you to get Blake!' And all this while she's slapping him in the face, attempting to revive him for her own wicked ends.

Meanwhile, at the Kasses' apartment in Century City, besides a residual dragging of one foot and a problem with her speech, Katy was making almost miraculous progress on her road to recovery. It was February of 1982 and Katy begged Joan not to divorce Ron, and she promised to try. They went to a marriage counselor. Joan continued to work as hard as she could, on *Dynasty* and other projects, She appeared in a made-for-TV movie titled *Paper Dolls*, which served as the basis for the ABC-TV series—the latter obviously without Joan. Next came the British-made *Nutcracker*, in which Joan played the principal of a ballet school, somehow managing to wind up in a bubble bath and between satin sheets. (Look, when you're hot, you're hot.) While she was in London, Joan granted an interview to a reporter from the *Sunday Times*. He was particularly taken with the coldness between the Kasses: 'They spoke to each other at the impersonal level of a desk intercom,' he reported. Asked by her publicity man whether or not Ron was home, Joan replied, 'He's in the house, I think.' Fewer roses than ever were coming up at the Kasses', but good to her word to Katy, Joan persevered. Throughout this difficult period Joan kept up a good front, especially with the press. She simply denied that there were any problems between her and Ron. In a *People* magazine article in December, Joan was asked point blank about her marriage, and the fact that Ron had moved out, briefly, a few months earlier. 'I just needed a little space,' she responded. 'We're both mature adults. Sure we have problems. ... We *do* spend a lot of time apart. ... I mean, we aren't exactly teenagers anymore.' It was a very well thought out argument, but it was a lie. She was lying selflessly, for Katy's sake.

In the late seventies, once again needing money, Joan had made a movie called *Homework*, a sex comedy that was so weedy and unimportant that the distributors had never released it in the United States. Of course, in 1982, when Joan suddenly became 'hot' and sensational box office, they reconsidered. Joan's appearance in the film lasted for only a few minutes, but she was being billed above the title. Furthermore, a double had stood in for her during a couple of nude scenes. The ads that the company, Farley Pictures, used to blitz the media implied that the body belonged to Joan (in fact she did no nude scenes for this movie), and Joan sought a restraining order to half the ads and the distribution of the film on the grounds that the campaign was 'false and misleading'. The company changed the ad, but Joan continued her suit, and reportedly received a $10,000 settlement. She was letting it be known that she was not a lady to be tricked and used - any exploitation would come from her from now on, not from others.

Feeling litigious, Joan attempted, in November, to stop 'a weekly paper from printing a story based on her sizzling memoirs' as the *New York Post* reported it. The judge this time denied the temporary restraining order. Joan had, after all, written the words herself, and her decision to stop the book's publication in the United States had been an afterthought.

13
Overnight Sensation

In December Joan was invited to be mistress of ceremonies at a benefit concert in London, in front of Queen Elizabeth and Prince Philip. A week before the benefit the *Daily News* reported in a small item that the 'phone and electricity [have been] shut off in her swank Mayfair pad in London for non-payment of utility bills'. The London tabloids gave it far greater attention. When Joan was about to enter the Royal Albert Hall for rehearsals, she was served with a writ for the nonreturn of a car British Leyland had loaned her eighteen months before in exchange for some ads she had done for them. Joan couldn't have cared less about the car – in fact she thought it was a gift and hadn't used it anyway – but the publicity surrounding the by now wealthy star's inability to pay her bills enraged her. Embarrassed not only for herself, but for the Queen and Prince Philip, who had invited her to oversee the very prestigious concert, Joan knew precisely where the blame lay. With Ron. He had been in charge of paying bills, but as in the past, he was being incredibly lackadaisical about his duties. Once again, Joan realized that she had to get out of the marriage, Katy or not. But still, she waited and tried.

A month later, on the *Dynasty* set, Joan became ill. She was rushed to the hospital, and after extensive tests her illness was diagnosed as gastroenteritis, a condition normally associated with extreme stress. She was released and got home to find Ron asleep. He was in a deep sleep, and try as she might, Joan couldn't wake him up. It was the final straw. She decided then and there that they had to separate. Finally they did.

Ironically, as the separation was taking effect, *Good Housekeeping* ran the sweetest three-page spread on the Kasses and their seventeen-room home in Beverly Hills. To look at the pictures one would presume that the American Dream had come true, and a flicker of envy would enter even the most skeptical, cynical mind. The moral, as always, is that it is never good to believe anything one reads.

With the final dissolution of her marriage and with *Dynasty* in the top-ten rated shows on television, Joan has become practically public property. A week didn't go by when she wasn't the subject of a newspaper item or magazine article (and still doesn't). She was nominated for a Golden Globe Award as Best Actress in a television series in 1982 and 1983, and won the second time around. Among her other words at her acceptance speech were 'I would like to thank Sophia Loren for turning down the part.' Even her sense of humour was finally being used in the right places and at the right times.

There were very few things Joan hadn't done professionally in her thirty years in show business by 1982, and making a film for children was one of them. She got her opportunity when actress Shelley Duvall approached her to play the role of the mother and the wicked witch in Showtime's Faerie Tale Theatre production of *Hansel and Gretel*. There was a wonderful irony to the beautiful star being made up to look hideous, and the warts, large hooked nose, filthy teeth and hair, and green skin that were added to Joan's face really gave kids a scare and managed to shock their parents at the same time. Her performance was a nasty, amusing gem, and she was nominated by the National Cable Television Association for Best Actress. Witch or bitch, Joan was coming out on top.

Early in 1983 Joan left her agent, Tom Korman, who had convinced her to do *Dynasty*, and signed with the powerful William Morris Agency. Huge stars need huge organizations behind them, and William Morris and Joan have become a perfect match. Since then she has signed a million-dollar deal with Revlon to promote their new fragrance *Scoundrel* (once again, quite a change in attitude from the woman who said she would feel like a 'hypocrite' doing commercials), as well as completing another contract to appear in ads for Cannon towels.

In truth, there is very little hypocrisy here; both of these products suggest glamor. Joan is finally being marketed properly, simply because for the first time in her career she is marketing herself, and not permitting others to make her decisions for her.

In the middle of 1983 Joan met thirty-six-year-old Peter Holm, a former pop star and current businessman. Their friendship was clearly a close one but with Joan's new-found sense of security she is unlikely to allow herself to become completely dependent on any one man. On the other hand Joan always enjoys the company of an intelligent, entertaining and goodlooking sparring partner.

What else was left? Fifty movies, numerous television guest shots, a starring role on one of television's hottest shows, a young lover, three marriages, three children, money pouring in (about $50,000 an episode for *Dynasty*), apparent happiness at last. Where was 'Britain's Bad Girl', the 'pouty panther' that behaved rebelliously and made people sit up and listen and always had one more surprise up her sleeve? She wasn't dead yet.

At the age of fifty Joan decided to pose nude for *Playboy* magazine, most of whose previous models had been born around the time Joan was marrying for the second time, and for whom Richard Nixon was the first president not to be seen as a historical figure.

'Everybody says, "Oh, Joan, shocking girl. There she goes again, always doing the wrong thing, always shocking everybody and being controversial," ' Joan has been quoted as saying. And not only is it true, it's impossible to believe that Joan doesn't love the notoriety.

Joan managed to convince herself that posing in the nude for *Playboy* would somehow advance the feminist movement, which, she says, 'is involved not just in equal pay but in proving that a woman can be attractive at any age'. Her politics may be a bit cloudy, but the effect has been anything but negative.

Not only has the *Playboy* spread increased her popularity (men, who normally don't watch soap operas, have begun watching *Dynasty*, and it probably isn't the plot that keeps them glued to their sets), but she and *Playboy* have received hundreds, if not thousands, of letters agreeing that it has done wonders for women over a 'certain age', encouraging them to flaunt it if they've got it. 'I'm far too vain, I've too much pride, and I'm much too intelligent to stand there with fat arms and a big fat belly. To me,' she adds, 'I've got a great body. Sometimes it looks terrific and if it's photographed right, it can look absolutely great.' Once again Joan is marketing herself brilliantly. The entire package she has decided on to present to the public is exquisitely wrapped. Not to be mercenary, not to be too calculating, Joan also realized that posing for *Playboy* would be fun.

'I thought, fuck it, what the hell?' Spoken like a true star of the eighties. 'I didn't set out to be any of this. I didn't set out to be an over-forty sex symbol. But I've always had a very good inner voice, and I also believe that a person who has never made a mistake never accomplishes much.'

14
Jackie

Conspicuously, peculiarly, and apparently deliberately absent from Joan's own memoir, *Past Imperfect*, and from most of Joan's interviews is her sister, Jackie. Less than five years younger than Joan (although her fudging about her age has become somewhat of a joke by now – she managed to become two years younger than she was in 1978 by the time she gave an interview in 1980), Jackie is, at this point, probably richer than and almost as famous as Joan. One can surmise from *Past Imperfect* that when Jackie was a teenager she was jealous of Joan – and idolized her. She listened in on her older sister's phone conversations, Elsa Collins has written, and she begged Joan for news of Hollywood, her own particular 'promised land'. Joan never returned to London without gifts for Jackie, and she was concerned enough to ask Jackie to 'pray' for her when she wanted a part in *The Opposite Sex*. Jackie stood by Joan's side when Joan was fighting for her divorce from Maxwell Reed, and Joan played hostess at Jackie's wedding. They finally collaborated on *The Stud*, when Joan asked Jackie to write the screenplay, something Jackie had never attempted before. Jackie came to Hollywood when she was still in her teens to be near Joan, but by 1960 she was 'sick and tired' of being known only as Joan's little sister. She changed her name twice to help gain her own identity, to be free of whatever influence Joan's career might have had on hers.

'You know,' Joan said recently, 'Jackie's book *Hollywood Wives* was a best seller and I'm one of the most popular TV actresses. What do you suppose the odds are that two English sisters would make it this big here in America, where the competition is so fierce? I'd say billions to one! I think that had a lot to do with how our father and mother brought us up, don't you think? It wasn't just in the genes.'

Personalities aren't mentioned. 'They're not bitchy toward each other,' says 'a family friend', quoted in *Cosmopolitan* magazine, 'but there's a definite rivalry – a friendly competition.' Jackie, sounding as if she and Joan had rehearsed their lines together, says, 'It's wonderful when two offspring from the same family become famous and successful. ... One of us might say something in print that might offend the other. So Joan and I recently reached agreement that we'll not comment about each other, even though there's nothing I could say that's critical or bitchy in any way. I admire Joan enormously.' What comes to mind here is the far more off-the-cuff statement Jackie had made years earlier that Joan was always best in movies 'playing bitches'. The impression one is left with, judging from Joan's recent attributable comments about Jackie and vice versa, is closer to the relationship between, say the USSR and the United States than it is to two sisters. Detente exists between the Collins girls.

On the other hand, in a 1983 article in *McCall's*, a 'close relative' is quoted as saying about Joan, 'It's not that she's rude. She just gets to the point of things fast. ... She's *such* a survivor that she makes the puzzling out of who she really is the *other* person's problem.' Who could this 'close relative' be? Joe Collins, at eighty-one, has never been one to chat with the press, even in England. Their brother, Bill, has never been interviewed by the press. Children don't speak about their mother that way at the age of eleven (even presuming the press could get to Katy, which they couldn't), and Tara and Sacha are away at school and have never been known to give information about their parents to anyone. The quote seems to be competitive; it is a very personal statement. In short, the statement of a sister who, for many years, saw herself being compared to and in awe of someone she simply couldn't be, and furthermore, couldn't figure out.

Joan was so beautiful that strangers wanted to kiss her. Jackie had her nose redone many years ago. Joan eventually succeeded in the movie business; Jackie got out after many years of making movies that didn't even get her in the fan magazines. They both have claimed to have been thrown out of school at fifteen for smoking – which one actually owns that particular piece of notoriety? Jackie has worn pants (in contrast to skirts or dresses), and pants alone, since 1972; Joan succeeded brilliantly at cheesecake photos, and still does. Could this be the desire of a younger sibling to maintain her identity over the older? Jackie's relationship with their mother was far closer than Joan's – this we learn from *Past Imperfect*. Joan wishes hers could have been closer, but we sense her sorrow, rather then her resentment, over the issue. Joan has always tried to please her father; Jackie waited until hours before her second marriage to inform him that it was taking place. Joan has always tried to 'find difficult men and make them love [her]'; Jackie has written books to, as she admits, 'get a dig at' men and to show them that they can't continue to treat women badly and not expect the same treatment in return. Joan has always found men who wanted to run her career, and indeed she always wanted to be taken care of (she reports that her psychiatrist told her that she was 'still looking to conquer Daddy'); Jackie married a man twenty years her senior who convinced her that she would finish her first novel, a decision that changed her life. When asked about Joan's forthcoming autobiography, Jackie said that she probably wouldn't get around to hers until she's ninety.

What one senses, given these facts and hearing what these two remarkable women have to say, is that Joan, despite her problems and insecurities, has remained the more vulnerable of the Collins sisters. Whereas Joan remains overly optimistic about almost everything, Jackie continues to write books about role reversal that are patently man-hating. Joan has always known how beautiful she was, but she never had control over using her beauty until recently. Jackie (particularly with her original nose) had a lot to compete with in her older sister: a gorgeous child, a young woman who was voted the most beautiful girl in England, a face that appeared on the cover of magazines from the time she was seventeen – in short, a star. Joan could remain sweet; once she left home there was no one to compete with. Jackie, on the other hand, was constantly reminded, if not by her parents, then by the newspapers and magazines she read. Jackie became angry, or at least acknowledged her anger at some point, and took matters into her own hands.

There had been too many upsetting incidents for her to be able simply to forget. She became angry, for example, with Hollywood producers who wanted to seduce her in exchange for parts in movies, so she wrote a book (or two) about them. She was angry about the way Hollywood treated her, and she exposed that treatment in another book. Jackie says that she finds writing more fulfilling than acting because with writing 'each book develops into something, but with acting there is never really a completion'. At least there wasn't, one might add, in *her* acting experience. 'It is soul-destroying when you are supposed to be good-looking and have a good figure, to be exploited purely for that,' Jackie has said in commenting about how fortunate she was, in a way, to have gotten out of the 'whole starlet world'. Whose soul is she comparing hers to? One wonders. She said, in 1969, that she 'loved' the way the film companies were 'queuing up to buy [her] books at a fabulous price' and that she had had 'the greatest pleasure' in turning down film parts offered her since she became famous as an author. When asked by her father 'why not write a decent book under the family name?' Jackie (obviously unlike Joan, who had been concerned about her father's reactions to her nudity in *The Stud*) replied defiantly and independently: 'I wouldn't make any money that way.'

With regard to her always wearing pants, Jackie has said: 'Some people may think I don't have legs; that's their problem, not mine.' With regard to raising her children, she has said: 'My children come everywhere with me'; this, too, is to be compared with the fact that Joan's children were frequently in boarding schools. Finally, there is the veiled threat directed toward Joan in a *People* magazine article that ran in August of 1979: 'Sister Joan,' the article states, 'may be a character in yet another book. I'm not sure we'll be on speaking terms afterward," Jackie worries. "You have to include warts and all."'

If Joan's motivations in life can be summed up as a desire to be loved by everyone in the world, particularly Daddy, then one would sum up Jackie's motivations in terms of revenge – revenge particularly aimed at Hollywood, Joan, and anyone else who ever in any way rejected her. Now that she is in her late forties (despite her avowals to the contrary), she, like Joan, has taken control of her life and, like Scarlett O'Hara, 'will never go hungry again', emotionally or otherwise.

Jackie's books today are immediate best sellers. They are referred to by reviewers as 'nasty', 'foulmouthed', and 'out to shock', and have blazed a trail previously only traveled by male writers, who, Jackie says, write more like 'gynecologists'.

In short, it seems as if the Collins sisters (another tag Jackie deplores) don't like each other very much. 'When I stopped acting and started to write, the tag [Joan Collins's little sister] went away – like that!' Jackie told the *Daily News* in September 1979. And Joan, asked by *People* magazine in December 1982 about the demands on her time that *Dynasty* makes, explained, 'I've given up going to the gym and reading crap fiction.'

15

Superstardom

When Joan worked on Twentieth Century-Fox's lot in the fifties, Marilyn Monroe was a superstar. Monroe, in fact, was that studio's only superstar. She died, in her prime, in 1962. Psychologists are quick to point out that young people, unformed personalities, and people who have not matured take poorly to superstardom and frequently destroy themselves. Getting through life, the psychologists claim, is difficult enough without having the whole world taking note of one's every move. There is the tendency to want more than one can possibly handle, like the child who eats forty chocolate chip cookies simply because they're there and no adult is around to stop him. The pursuit of pleasure can be self-destructive, particularly if one is immature and has no perspective as to what real pleasure is all about.

Joan does not fit into this category, either as a person or as a superstar. She has spent thirty-five years waiting for something like her current success to happen, and she always knew what the odds were. She claims she never really wanted to be a 'star', but one can only assume that either she was covering herself psychologically because she felt she would never achieve it anyway, or the type of 'star' she had in mind didn't exist for her to aspire to. If you are wise and a superstar, you use the complete freedom you have to make certain that you get not only what you have always wanted but what is good for you. This is the category Joan falls into.

In addition, your personality doesn't change and you don't abuse your position. On the brink of superstardom, in March of 1982, Joan was the subject of a lengthy *Daily News* interview. In it she said, 'You know, I'm really a very cautious person. I have been hurt a lot by being too optimistic. I went around telling everybody I was going to play Cleopatra – I tested for it six times. And then, of course, Elizabeth Taylor got the part.' Learning from experience is one way to assure happiness, and Joan was making certain she didn't make the same mistake twice, despite the fact that the word of her 'magnetism' on *Dynasty* was out. Earlier in the interview Joan explained, 'I think I have my priorities right: first and foremost my children, then my husband [she and Ron were still trying to work things out at the time], and my career.' Stardom was not uppermost in her mind and she was not going to be moved by the prospect of it showing up on her doorstep. She knows that it is totally ephemeral and realizes that she's 'America's brunette flavor of the month'. When Barbara Walters, in April of 1984 (by which time the word *superstar* had practically taken on a new luster in Joan's case), busied herself with trying to grease Joan out of her chair with the question 'The fame, the excitement ... are you afraid that someday it will all be over?' Joan gazed coolly at her and said, 'No, because I *know* it will be.' And she meant it. She had been around too long, had had the guts to keep fighting precisely enough to keep her career alive when her earlier star was on the wane, and had seen too many people destroyed by their own self-delusions to think that her current success could last forever.

What is it like to work with Joan, now that she can call the shots, now that she doesn't have to dress up as a Valentine or

Thanksgiving turkey when the studio heads tell her to? In the middle of a grueling photography shoot, *Rolling Stone* reported in March 1984, Joan was asked, while dressed like a 'cycle slut – black leather jacket and all,' to get into a position she would have found uncomfortable. 'My days of torturing myself are over, boys. I don't want to do any kinky weirdness. You have your fun with your models,' she said. No more Thanksgiving birds for Joan, unless she wants to do one.

On the other hand, on the set of *Dynasty*, despite the critics' claims that she is the reason for the show's success, she never acts like a prima donna. True, she gets to approve any costume Alexis is slated to wear, and only Alexis can wear certain designer clothes (the show's weekly clothing budget is close to $20,000!), but Joan is an *actress* with her colleagues, and not the *star* of the show in her attitude toward them. 'She stimulated the set when she was added,' says Linda Evans. 'Joan has a wonderful working mind. You know sparks will fly when she's out there. She adds a splash of sauce,' adds John James, who plays Jeff Colby. Lynn Loring, a vice-president at Aaron Spelling Productions, has even higher praise: 'Joan is not only an excellent actress, but one of the most professional I've ever worked with,' Loring told *McCall's* in November of 1983. 'She's never late. She does not have a temper. She gives an enormous amount to the other actors. She's straight, gutsy – a terrific broad in the best sense of the word.' As if to prove the point, at the end of the luncheon interview session with *McCall's*, Joan realized she was going to be late to the set. 'They'll kill me if I'm late,' she said. 'Can you drop me at the set? Let's go – fast!'

Is her ego so inflated that she thinks, as the reviewers do, that she has made the show a success and that Alexis is a particularly challenging, difficult role? Not at all. 'Roles of this kind are genuinely fun to do,' she told the *Daily News* at the end of 1981. 'What I'm really trying to do is bring to television the outrageously glamorous women we always saw in films,' in other words the stars of yesterday whom Joan herself always admired. And as to the difficulty in playing Alexis, Joan says merely, 'It's easy to play a bitch' and 'any actress would have the same impact.' Well, maybe and maybe not. For example, Margaret Rutherford, a wonderful actress, would have made a lousy Alexis. Joan is selling herself short here, but curbing her natural optimism is another way of making sure she survives. It's true that the lines are well written, but the special combination of elegance, deadliness, and articulateness that Joan brings to the role makes it an important part rather than a caricature of evil.

Does she have any delusions about the part? Is it the be-all and end-all of her career dreams? '*Dynasty* is the highest peak I've had in my life, professionally and in terms of public acceptance,' she told the British magazine *Woman's Own* in May 1983. 'It's not *Brideshead Revisited*, in the sense of great television, but what we're doing is what actors used to do in weekly rep – entertain. The series is good for my career, my popularity, and,' she adds, 'the money' (which is, by the way, reported to be $1.5 million a year). In December 1982 she confessed to still looking forward to 'that one really good modern woman's role', and later told *Cosmopolitan*, 'Theater is like my annuity. I know it's always there, even if *Dynasty* stops tomorrow. I'll travel England and America for the rest of my life, getting back to what I wanted to do initially. Television makes you a celebrity, nationally known, and the audience-recognition factor is my ace in the hole.' A good card player knows the value of an ace in the hole, and has no delusions.

Another ace in the hole, despite her enormous salary and Revlon contract, is a brand-new line of affordable jewelry that she agreed to endorse in August of 1984 for a company called Design Lines, Inc. She doesn't actually design the jewelry herself, but has a say in what it looks like. It's the perfect tie-in for her upcoming NBC-TV movie *The Cartier Affair*. Joan is making all of the facts of her career work in unison, thereby upping the chances for an ace in the hole. She has the sort of confidence that comes with age, not stardom. 'I spent my life being told what to do by people who shouldn't have been directing traffic, let alone my life,' she recently told *Us* magazine, her wit laced with more than a little anger. Her success has allowed her to 'get involved in other creative endeavors', she added.

What about her looks, her life-style, her taste in clothes? At 5′ 6″, 120 pounds, she is built precisely the way she was twenty-five years ago. Although she has had a gym installed in her home, she thinks the Jane Fonda workout is 'a bit of a hype'. She, herself, does fifty sit-ups, twenty-five push-ups, and works out with weights for about fifteen minutes a day. Her face is still as beautiful as it ever was, if not more so, but *Rolling Stone*, in an article noticeable in its consistent snideness, says that from a distance of twelve inches she does look beautiful, but 'from any closer, she looks a bit ... rough. Her makeup is like a mask ... her lashes stand out like awnings.' Most of us will never get close enough to notice. She is opposed to cosmetic surgery and has never had any performed on her. She became very angry a few years ago when ex-sexpot Brigitte Bardot was quoted, at forty-nine, as saying 'I won't be seen in a bikini because nobody wants to see me. My flesh is rotting.' 'I don't think women should think that way about themselves,' Joan commented. Either great pride or great disgust in anything as tangible as looks is not what Joan believes in.

She lives in a three-level, seventeen-room house in Beverly Hills with daughter Katy (Tara and Sacha are away at school) and, as of this writing, with Peter Holm (with whom, *Us* magazine reports, she is said to be making wedding plans). The ten months during which she lived alone (after Ron and before Peter) were very happy times for her. She told *Cosmopolitan* that she loves her life, she makes her own decisions, and she's 'not living through a man for the first time since [she] was seventeen years old'. She goes out frequently, still loves to party and hates to be unescorted, but often stays home with Katy, 'eating dinner ... playing Monopoly and watching reruns of *The Brady Bunch*'. She owns a Rolls-Royce, has a wicked taste for beluga caviar, and Louis Roederer Cristal champagne, and wears plenty of jewelry, sometimes real, sometimes fake (much of which was stolen in the south of France in July of 1983). She recently returned from Paris with matching diamond bracelets for herself and Katy. She won't take drugs; reportedly having tried cocaine once in St Tropez in the sixties and hating the experience was enough. She won't smoke marijuana, not only because when she has tried it, it has had a bad effect on her, but because she's terrified of catching herpes. She's convinced that 'herpes and AIDS have come as the great plagues to teach us all a lesson' about sexual freedom.

She dresses in clothes that make her look and feel her best, whether they're in fashion or not. That's just one way in which she differs from Alexis. 'I think women who slavishly follow fashion are pathetic,' she says with great verve. 'Alexis is a bit pathetic; the fact that she always has to have a new dress for every scene.' In addition, as Joan has said elsewhere, Alexis isn't a survivor, and she is.

What about other stars? Who are they? 'Movie stars aren't where it's at today,' she told *Playboy*, and named Tom Selleck and Larry Hagman as the successors to Brando with regard to stardom. Also with regard to Hagman, her rival in TV villainy, she said 'I met [him] the other day ... and [he] was talking like and acting like the character he plays. He was just so overbearing and so stupid, using a phony accent. ...' Hagman, by the way, reacted fast to this criticism, telling Liz Smith in the *Daily News*, that it's 'too bad she can't handle success as well as I can'. Somehow, that doesn't seem to be the point.

And since certain things don't change, Joan, even in her recently found superstardom, still tends to be better than her material. She was recently the subject of a Dean Martin roast on television, and sat poised with charm, elegance, and humor while a group of comedians took potshots at her sexuality and the image she portrays.

The effect she has had as Alexis is astounding. She gets over 12,000 letters a week, most of them loving and hating her at the same time. 'Alexis' as a name for newborn girls has leaped from the low nineties to the top twenty in popularity. In a recent poll taken in England, Joan says, she was voted the world's second most powerful woman, placing right after Margaret Thatcher.

This kind of fame is so staggering that it's a good thing it has happened when it has and not when Joan was an impressionable young starlet. She is still learning about herself (as we all continue to do throughout our lives if we're smart). 'I'm more complex than I thought,' she said recently. 'The compartment that's easy to put me in is "freethinking, sexy broad with a dirty mouth, who pretty much does what she wants.' But there's more to me than that.'

At this stage in her life and her career, she actually *can* do what she wants, and she does. But she's right; there's more to her than that.